to Bless Your Home and Family

Keeping loved ones close to God

and each other through the holidays

ADVENTIST FAMILY TRADITIONS

Edited by Jerry D. Thomas
Designed by Michelle C. Petz
Cover photos © PhotoDisc Inc.
Cover illustration (photo composite) by Michelle C. Petz

Printed in the United States of America

Library of Congress Cataloging-in-Publication Data:

ISBN 0-8163-1797-6

00 01 02 03 04 • 5 4 3 2 1

Contents

Dedication

To my family, who has made Christmas a time of traditions, warmth, and love.

Thank you, Darrell, Peg, Darin, Rod, Dawn, and Judy.

A special "Thank You" to Kyle and Tiffany for making Christmas fun.

Kyle, thank you for telling Grandma, "Just do it, Grandma. Just do it!"

A Special Thanks

A special thanks to each one of you who contributed your stories and shared your family Christmas traditions and fun stories. Thank you to the students of Sandy Daniels and Joan Johnson who wrote what Christmas means to them. You are the ones who have made this book a reality. You have demonstrated the true spirit of Christmas giving.

Introduction

Christmas and families—the traditional pictures of holiday happiness and joy seem to always include a gathering of family. Most of us can identify with these scenes, at least in some of our memories. Sadly, this hasn't always been true for everyone. If you grew up in those families without warm holiday memories, my heart goes out to you. But you can change that for yourself and those you love starting this year.

It is my hope that each person who reads this book will find ways to strengthen their family bonds by observing Christmas traditions. If no traditions have been handed down through the generations to you, begin to build your own.

There is hope for everyone who wants to change their life patterns and chooses to make a difference in their family. Being a member of a loving family is the most wonderful thing on this earth. Jeremiah 29:11 says, "For I know the thoughts that I think toward you, says the Lord, thoughts of peace and not of evil, to give you a future and a hope" (NKJV). I believe God wants us to experience the joy of genuine love in our families. May this be your experience from this day forward.

Hearts Come Home for Christmas

by Dawn and Evelyn Glass

Thoughts turn to home at Christmas
Remembering the happy times, the laughter,
Family and friends who came each day.
We long to return to those days that were.

The warm kitchen with its delicious smell,
Inviting us to come and be favored,
With lefsa just coming off the grill,
Ready to be buttered and savored.

Cookies waiting to be decorated,
Pumpkin pie with its aroma of spice,
And cranberry sauce sweet and red,
Made being there especially nice.

The big green tree with lights aglow,
And boughs hung with glittering balls,
Rocking horses, tinsel and chains,
Welcomed us down the halls.

Under the tree were many packages,
Decorated with ribbons and bows.
There is at least one for me, surely,
For this is home, where love shows.

All hearts come home for Christmas,
Even if just for a moment when alone.
To think again of all that was special
When we were all together at home.

"So a man's heart reveals the man"

(PROVERBS 27:19).

TUGS ON OUR HEARTSTRINGS

Christmas creates a special longing within each of us, a feeling that is sometimes hard to identify. It is a craving for a time that is long past, a time when we were children. It creates a tug on our heartstrings as we turn our thoughts toward home and the memories we share with our family.

I remember the first time I saw the elaborate holiday decorations in our local department store window. Tugging on the hands of my mom and dad, I wriggled with excitement. The bright colors, the animated Christmas figures, the glittering snowflakes, and the toys carefully placed where a child could see them fascinated me. The thought of Christmas was almost too much to comprehend. Excitement was everywhere.

At times, we all ache to live again in those days in our memories—days when happiness seemed to flow over our families. Time itself seemed to slow down as the family celebrated Christmas. The warmth of those memories can engulf us in a moment, tugging our hearts back home as we reminisce of days gone by.

Our memories include a house full of grandparents, aunts, uncles, and cousins who came to share the joy of the season on Christmas Eve and again on Christmas Day. Each one was special and all are remembered for their individual mannerisms and characteristics. The ones who spent time playing with the children made the day special for us.

Many of the Christmas traditions our grandparents and parents shared with us were handed down by earlier generations. I have shared them with my family also, because families where traditions are observed are healthy families.

Traditions are the warp and weft upon which our most precious memories are woven. Those who have studied the family tell us that traditions make a difference in our lives by creating and fortifying our emotional security. Children from homes with strong traditions have a sense of family unity. Some studies have shown that those families with the most traditions have the strongest family ties. They are the homes that children love to return to.

I invite you to spend a few hours reading and experiencing the spirit of the season. Come with me as we take a peek at the traditions that are being observed in homes each Christmas season. Allow your heart to come home for Christmas, if only in memory.

Christmas is for kids . . .

"My favorite thing to do on Christmas Eve is sing songs. The first song we sing is 'Away in a Manger.' That is my favorite song to sing. The first, second, and third verses go like this:

1. 'Away in a manger no crib for a bed. The little Lord Jesus asleep on his head.
2. The stars in the sky look where he lay the little Lord Jesus asleep on the hay.
3. The cattle are lowing, the poor baby wakes. But little Lord Jesus no crying He makes.'

So there's the song of 'Away in a Manger.' I like that song because it is about how Christ was born."

—Brianna Nieto, Fifth Grade

"She brought forth her firstborn son, and wrapped him in swaddling clothes, and laid Him in a manger; because there was no room for them in the inn"

(LUKE 2:7, KJV).

THE BIRTH THAT TOUCHED HEARTS

"And there were in the same country shepherds abiding in the field, keeping watch over their flock by night. And, lo, the angel of the Lord came upon them, and the glory of the Lord shone round about them: and they were sore afraid. And the angel said unto them, Fear not: for, behold, I bring you good tidings of great joy, which shall be to all people. For unto you is born this day in the city of David a Saviour, which is Christ the Lord" (Luke 2: 8-11, KJV).

The shepherds were resting that evening as they quietly watched their sheep. They were among the few faithful Jews who were looking for the Messiah. In the still evening air, they listened to the sounds of their sheep in the fold. This was a time that they could relax, sit, and talk around their fire.

Suddenly an angel of the Lord appeared with glory that lit up the sky. As this glory shone and momentarily blinded them, the shepherds were frightened. With great joy, the angel announced the birth of Jesus and told them where to find the Baby. The angel was then joined by a multitude of heavenly hosts who proclaimed, "Glory to God in the highest, and on earth peace, good will toward men."

What a glorious night! The angels in all their glory filled the sky with brightness and beautiful colors! Often I try to picture in my mind what the sky looked like that night so long ago. How did the angels appear as they spoke and sang? Were they in straight rows or in a semicircle like a choir, or were they just one big group?

Living in the northern United States, we are often privileged to see the aurora borealis or the "Northern Lights" as we commonly call them. When it happens, the northern sky is alight with color. Electrical particles form a sheer curtain that waves and moves in the sky. The red, green, and gold colors glow with a shimmering beauty like no other. I have often wondered if this display resembles the sky the night the angels appeared to the shepherds as they watched their sheep that night so long ago.

We can be certain that the coming of our Lord to this earth was the cause for a scene of unrivaled beauty when the angels announced His birth to the shepherds. There was color and beauty displayed in a momentous way by God, the Creator of color and beauty. Is it any wonder that at the Christmas season we enjoy the beauty of bright, vibrant colors and lights as we celebrate the birth of Jesus?

The angelic voices were melodious and clear as they brought tidings of the arrival of Baby Jesus. There must have been joyous music accompanying this announcement. The shepherds were attracted by the glory of this wonderful announcement filling the air with praise and joy.

The shepherds must have been amazed and overwhelmed by the sight and sound of the angels. But they quickly decided to go and find the Baby Jesus and worship Him. When they found the little family in the stable with the Babe lying in the manger, they bowed down and worshiped Him. Leaving this awesome scene, they told all they met about the wonderful things that had happened to them that evening. They were filled with praise and glorified God as they returned to care for their sheep.

Thinking of that scene on that long ago evening when animals and humans were quietly living in close proximity gives one a sense of peace. The glories that were displayed as the angels made their announcement have never been surpassed. The atmosphere felt by the shepherds as they witnessed the scene around the manger generated a peace in their hearts. This peace touches our hearts and brings hope to us all. History does not record the exact date of Christ's birth so mankind has chosen to remember it on the eve of December 24.

On December 17 in the year 1889, a wise lady wrote "What matchless love Jesus has manifested for a fallen world! If angels sung because the Saviour was born in Bethlehem, shall not our hearts echo the glad strain, Glory to God in the highest, peace on earth, good will to men? Although we do not know the exact day of Christ's birth, we would honor the sacred event. May the Lord forbid that anyone should be so narrow-minded as to overlook the event because there is an uncertainty in regard to the exact time. Let us do what we can to fasten the minds of the children upon those things which are precious to everyone who loves Jesus.

Let us teach them how Jesus came into the world to bring hope, comfort, peace and happiness to all. The angels explained the reason of their great joy, saying, 'For unto you is born this day in the city of David a Saviour, which is Christ the Lord'" (EGW, RH).

Fitting advice for us today also.

Today we celebrate Christmas Eve and Christmas Day because we, too, are filled with the joy of knowing Jesus Christ came to this earth as a baby to live and die for all of us. Each family has its own traditions made up of rituals, decorations, foods, and gatherings that they observe each year. Share the excitement and joy of many families and the traditions they observe as you read this book.

CHRISTMAS IS FOR KIDS . . .

"I enjoy Christmas shopping with my mom. After the presents are bought, she helps me wrap them."

—Eric Daniels, First Grade

"Our children have learned to regard Christmas as a day of rejoicing, and we should find it a difficult matter to pass over this holiday without some attention. It may be made to serve a good purpose"

(EGW, RH, December 15, 1885).

Days of Planning

Like other families of my generation and many youngsters of today, the kids in my neighborhood anxiously awaited the Christmas catalogs that arrived early in November. With the catalogs in hand, we could finally begin to think about the exciting days to come. We leafed slowly through the pages, pondering the wonders of the beautiful clothes and intriguing toys pictured there. We dreamed that maybe we might receive a new pair of slippers or a coat and at least one toy. If we could only receive a gift—any gift—complete happiness would be ours.

Along with dreaming of the things we would like, we carefully chose things for the other members of our family. Our ears were in tune to the wants of other members of our household. We knew that Christmas involved giving as well as getting.

Our mothers began to shop for the nuts, dried fruits, sugar, spices, and other ingredients to begin their Christmas baking. They baked for weeks before the big day. Freezers were not common in those days, so since the winters were cold, mothers took advantage of nature's deep freeze. To keep the treats fresh, they stored them in tins on the front porch or some other area of the house that was not heated.

Fathers would spend hours in the barn, basement, or garage building something special for their children. The dollhouses, wagons, and other treasures were constructed as near to the pictures in the catalogs as Dad could make them. Mother's knitting needles were always clicking as she made mittens, socks, and sweaters for her family. The sewing machine hummed swiftly along as the pieces of fabric became needed garments.

I think the planning was—and still is—as much a part of the excitement as celebrating the big day. The desire to demonstrate our love made us want to give gifts. We children entered into this aspect of Christmas preparation with an immeasurable amount of enthusiasm. Searching through the stores for just the right gift, we carefully spent our Christmas allowance on others.

Today children save their allowances and work extra jobs to have money to buy gifts. Some families help their children make special gifts. It all takes planning and makes the coming holiday exciting.

Ruth Johnson tells of the days when she was a child and how she planned for Christmas. Money was not very plentiful, but she was given a whole dollar to buy gifts for every member of her family. She says:

"There wasn't much money to spend in those days, but we always had a Christmas tree. I managed to stretch the dollar to buy gifts for everyone but one brother. So I drew his picture and put it in a frame and gave it to him. He didn't say much, but I doubt he appreciated it. Some gifts were homemade in those days."

Ingenuity helped Ruth stretch her dollar so she could buy gifts for everyone, and her creativity completed the gifts.

Very organized folks begin their Christmas shopping with the after-Christmas sales and continue on through the year choosing special gifts as they see them. Many men choose to wait until the week before Christmas to do their shopping. Early or late, shoppers all have their own methods of shopping and accomplish choosing their gifts in their own way.

The excitement of children is what makes Christmas shopping and gift-giving fun. They give us a perspective on Christmas that increases our enjoyment of the season. Christmas celebrations are for kids. Families that do not have little children often gather with those who do and enjoy the children of their brothers and sisters or friends. Without children, Christmas is not quite the same.

Christmas is for kids . . .

"My favorite thing to do at Christmas time is put up the Christmas tree. First my dad goes in the garage and gets the tree. After we get the tree out of the garage, we put it up. Then we put up the ornaments. We have made special ornaments at school each year. I like getting them out and putting them on the tree."

—*Krystle Haugen, Fourth Grade*

"Make . . . Christmas a blessing to yourselves and others" (GLORY TO GOD IN THE HIGHEST, P. 373).

CREATING THE ATMOSPHERE

When Darrell and I married, we chose to make Christmas a very special time for our family. At our house, the Christmas season seemed to officially begin when we brought the tree in to decorate it. Often the tree would have bits of snow left in its branches and we would carefully place it on a rug to thaw. With all of the snow thawed and the tree standing secure in its stand, we were ready to decorate.

We draped each branch with lights and ornaments collected through the years. It was, and still is, my responsibility to string the lights in place. Next came the treetop ornament in its place, then the rest of the ornaments and the tinsel were hung. We hung the unbreakable ornaments near the bottom of the tree. That way, if curious little hands should happen to touch and tug on them, no harm would come to the child or the ornaments.

I will always cherish the memories of the first time Peggy was old enough to hang the tinsel in place. Carefully, her little fingers placed the shiny ribbons on the branches. Each of our children created memories in our hearts as they excitedly helped decorate the tree from year to year.

Christmas trees hold a special fascination for little tots. Nine-month-old Rod was still in the crawling stage when he went over to investigate the shiny ornaments and, with a quick tug, brought the tree toppling over upon himself. A scared little boy was quickly comforted, and his tears ceased flowing. The fragments of a few broken balls were cleaned up, and a slightly disheveled tree was quickly righted. This event showed us the need for a new Christmas tradition—a hook in the ceiling above the tree with a fine wire reaching into the branches to hold it up firmly.

Over the years, we tried many different formulas to keep the trees moist and the needles intact throughout the season. Somehow they never seemed to do the trick. Too quickly, the trees lost their needles. We finally decided that perhaps the trees were too old by the time we bought them off the Christmas tree lot. We turned to a friend who could supply us with fresh cut trees. That was better, but it wasn't a permanent solution. Finally, we did the unthinkable and bought an artificial tree.

Rod, now old enough to be the chief tree assembler, was so efficient that I never learned how it all went together. When he left for the academy, I had to learn. Thankfully the directions were still intact, and I managed to do the job.

After a few years, Peg and Rod decided that Judy, our youngest, was a deprived child because she had never experienced Christmas with a "real tree." So off to the tree lot we went and purchased a real tree. The kids were excited and enjoyed the tree-trimming time. Alas, this tree also lost its needles too soon. There were needles all over the carpet—some even got woven into the fibers of the carpet. It seemed that we were vacuuming needles until the next Christmas.

We found, once again, that unless trees are fresh cut, the fragrance of pine—which we like so much—is absent and the tree never lasts as long as we wish. A real tree didn't seem so special after all, and we weren't able to keep it up as long as we liked. The next year, it was back to the artificial tree.

The tree with its lights all aglow is still the first thing our children look for when they arrive home for Christmas. Our tree has become the symbol that their home hasn't changed and that we are going to celebrate the holidays together.

Our tree is much the same each year. At the very top is a small angel with gossamer wings playing a violin. This gift from my mother-in-law is one of the little treasures I cherish. Among the other decorations are:

- Two filigree bells filled with angel hair given to us on our anniversary many years ago by Pauline and Bill
- A bell from the year of our country's bicentennial—a gift from Theresa
- The Santa made of yarn reminds us of Tara
- A little drummer boy made by Orlene
- A horse fashioned by Ann
- Macramé wreaths made by the Pathfinders
- Sparkly bead wreaths created by Judy
- Moravian stars made by Cheryl and Carol, Darrell's twin cousins
- and many other ornaments are reminders of friendship.

Each year we gave our children their own Christmas

ornaments to hang on the tree. When they started their own homes, these ornaments went with them. We still give each of them an ornament each year. Now our grandchildren are receiving ornaments from their parents each year, so the tradition continues.

We no longer hang tinsel on our tree. And the number of ornaments we hang has increased through the years. Still, each one is special and as each is placed dangling from a branch, we remember people, places, and special occasions. Our hearts are filled with warmth and love at tree-trimming time.

Brightly wrapped packages complete our holiday scene. Within each package is a gift chosen especially for the recipient. Of course some are disguised so the recipient can't guess what's inside. This tradition has continued through the years, as it adds an element of fun to gift opening time.

Arrangements appropriate to the season are placed on the tables and in other areas. A special arrangement for the dining table adds a bright spot to the room. Using dishes, glass balls, greenery, logs, and other ordinary objects makes it possible to create a beautiful piece that we enjoy through the season. Inexpensive small trees purchased at the craft store are decorated with mini ornaments and beads so each room can have a tree. Like the rest of the ornaments, we store these to be used year after year.

The house is filled with the fragrances of delicacies that we have learned to associate with the holiday season. These foods help to create happy mealtimes with all of the foods that have become traditional for our family. Meals prepared with love and anticipation have added to the joy of spending Christmas together.

Christmas, a family time filled with memories that tug at our heartstrings and give us a warm and loving feeling—Christmas, a time to build new memories and to cherish old ones.

Christmas is for kids . . .

"Christmas is not just a day to get presents but to honor the birth of our Savior and King. Christmas means eternal life for all of us, which is the most wonderful present anyone could give to you."

—Amy Pearce, Seventh Grade

"And when they had come into the house, they saw the young Child with Mary His mother, and fell down and worshiped Him. And when they had opened their treasures, they presented gifts to Him: gold, frankincense, and myrrh"

(MATTHEW 2:11, NKJV).

FOLLOWING THE EXAMPLE

The traditions of giving gifts to each other began with the visit of the wise men. They came bearing gifts that were befitting a king. Their expensive gifts held real meaning to the people of that time and culture. In Oriental lands, one would never think of paying a visit to a king without presenting a gift as an act of homage. The wise men had studied and planned for this trip. They knew their visit was to One of great position and honor. Guided by the star, they came bearing gifts that would be meaningful and useful to the family of the Son of God.

Most of us develop traditions with the gifts we give each year. For example, when our family was young, our children received slippers each Christmas. They looked forward to new slippers each Christmas Eve. When we shopped for slippers, we looked for ones that were unusual but serviceable. Slippers that resembled lions, tigers, cows, and other animals were favorites.

Before the days of electronic games and computers, children looked forward to simpler gifts. Often, enjoying the gifts meant braving the winter weather.

Candy Seltman writes of those days:

"Every Christmas morning, without fail, one could find us outdoors sliding down the hill on our new sled, with the snow and cold air blowing in our faces. Later, we were trying our new snowshoes, turning to examine our foot prints left behind in the new fallen snow. Sometimes we had to shovel the snow off the frozen creek to use our new skates.

"I remember hearing my mother express her delight over a glass plate my brother and I had deliberated over in the dime store. Today I enjoy using the same plate when I am entertaining.

"Opening the gifts and feeling the smooth texture of the paper and ribbon as we ripped through the paper or tissue to get to the gift and then holding it up to show everyone was also a gift.

"Another gift my dad gave to us each year was our Christmas Eve tour. Living in northern Minnesota, we would bundle up in our warm clothes and get in the Chevrolet to ride to town to see the lights on display. He drove the same route each year to the different communities in the area with we children happily expressing our excitement of the eve. There were times when we became very quiet as we all gazed out the windows, seeing the wonder of the electrical lights displayed on buildings and trees."

Growing up in Port Arthur, Ontario during the depression years, Pat Wangsnes remembers the lovely clothes her mother sewed for her and her four siblings. Often they were remade from clothes given by friends or neighbors. Always, they were appreciated.

Cindy Hall is a devoted aunt to her nieces, and she shares this experience:

"My nieces were probably three and four years old the Christmas it began. They considered pickles quite a delicacy. I decided their own personal jar of pickles might be a real treat so I wrapped a jar for each of them and placed them under the tree with their other presents. In the midst of toys and clothes and candy, I couldn't believe how their eyes lit up as they realized the whole jar was just for them—no sharing, and just maybe Mom would let them indulge whenever they wanted. I was glad I'd followed through with this off-the-wall idea.

"However, my joy didn't end there on Christmas morning. Imagine my surprise at the report our aunt gave after Sabbath School the following Sabbath. As the Cradle Roll teacher, she had asked each of the children to name their favorite Christmas present. One niece quickly replied, 'my favorite is the jar of pickles from my aunt.'

"Several years have passed and this tradition continues. Now I attempt to wrap them creatively, but they always guess as soon as they hear the slosh of the juice. Their eyes still dance with delight. My heart once again thanks God for the joy of simple gifts, special memories and traditions, and loved ones to share them with."

Kelly Sue Blake writes the story of how a tradition began with the birth of their first son.

"My first son was born on December 4. The ladies of my church had a baby shower for us just two weeks before Christmas. One gift in particular stands out in my memory. The woman who gave the gift came and sat beside me as I held it in my lap. It was beautifully wrapped and tied up in the ribbon, where a bow would ordinarily be, was a handmade, personalized Christmas tree ornament. She told me that every year she gave an ornament to each of her children. Knowing they would eventually leave home and start homes of their own, she wanted them to have their own ornaments to take with them that were a part of their family Christmas tradition.

"I thought this was such a lovely idea that I started doing that for my sons. Their Granny (my mother, Claudine Herber) thought this was such a wonderful tradition that she has been buying her grandchildren an ornament each year and presenting it to them as part of their birthday celebration. Now that my children are in school, they have been making Christmas ornaments in art class and these are also added to their respective collections. Each year there are three or four more ornaments added to this growing collection. It is with excitement that they hang 'their very own' ornaments on the tree as we get ready for Christmas."

My husband, Darrell, tells of the many Christmas boxes they received from Auntie Agnes. They especially liked her gifts because they were always toys. She didn't send clothes, and he and his brother, Virgil, thought that was very special. Even today, many years later, Auntie Agnes's love and thoughtfulness are not forgotten.

I have the same memories of my Auntie Marie and her traditional Christmas boxes filled with goodies. Candy was rarely seen in our house, and I was a typical child who loved candy. Imagine the thrill I had when I saw in her package to our family, a Fifth Avenue candy bar for each one of us! She also included many practical items we needed but remembered to fulfill some of our childish desires.

Giving gifts gives more joy to the giver than to the recipient.

Christmas is for kids . . .

"Christmas means family and friends from near and far. It means trees with presents under them, but most of all it is Jesus' birth. This is a special time of year.

"One time I saw an American girl doll, and I thought it would be fantastic to have one. I passed a few hints here and there and then forgot about it. On Christmas Eve, I opened a big package from Grandma, and I about exploded. There was an American girl doll named Kirsten! Her hair was braided, and she had on a pretty dress, and she was just beautiful! It was a wish that came true!

"Christmas is fun because I like to see the presents under the tree. It's fun to try and guess what is in all the packages. I like to see the expressions on people's faces when they open up a present from me. I also like to finally see what the presents under the tree really were."

–Becky Wicklund, Fourth Grade

"A merry heart does good like medicine"

(PROVERBS 17:22, NKJV).

MAKING GIFT EXCHANGES FUN

Shaking, lifting, prodding, prying, and feeling packages in an effort to find what is inside each one is part of the fun of Christmas for many people, including our oldest child. When she was a little girl, she was not above tearing a corner of the wrapping paper to get an extra hint about what was inside. It's all part of the excitement and fun of this season of celebration.

Thanks in large part to family curiosity, it became a part of our tradition to be creative in wrapping gifts, to disguise them beyond recognition. We created quite a number of tricks that were guaranteed to cause confusion for the curious.

- A brick included in the package gives extra weight.

- A few tins of food rolling around in a box create a real mystery about the gift inside.
- Boxes of various sizes and shapes are used to disguise the size of the present.
- Crumpled newspapers fill corners to hold objects stable in these bigger boxes.
- A few marbles left to rattle in the box add interest.
- Small cans of juice that will swish as you shake the package can add "sound effects" to the gift.

Various imaginative ideas have been utilized, all designed to keep the contents of the package secret.

Peggy reminded me that this practice began "because Dad was always so good at just looking at a box and knowing what was inside it."

One year I decided to give him a torque wrench. Now this is a rather special type of wrench and certainly not something I thought he would guess. I went to great lengths to keep it out of his sight until the moment he was to open it. I had his brother buy it. Then our sister-in-law wrapped it and put it under the tree. When he was handed the box, he picked it up and felt the weight of it and said, "Oh, a torque wrench."

I was flabbergasted! From that day forward, his gifts were disguised if we wanted to keep them a secret until he got them opened.

A favorite story we tell over and over involved a few tins of food from the pantry. The day before Christmas, I decided to make a casserole requiring one of these cans of food. I prepared everything that went in the dish and went to get the last ingredient, knowing I had the two cans in the pantry. But to my amazement, they weren't there. I asked everyone in the family if they had seen them. No one admitted that they knew anything about these cans.

At last Judy came up to me and whispered, "Mommy, I used them when I wrapped Daddy's package so he wouldn't be able to guess what's in the box." We had to chuckle as we unwrapped the gift and replaced one of the cans with something equally deceptive but less in demand. At Christmas time just asking, "What happened to the cans of soup or veggies?" begins a round of laughter from all of us.

A friend, DeAnn, has an extra measure of curiosity. She will go so far as to open a package to see what it contains and then rewrap it and place it back under the tree. When her family figured this out, they began to fill her packages with bits and pieces of various things and only bring the real gift out when it's time to open it.

With her infectious laugh, she told me about the first Christmas she and her husband shared after their wedding. The packages were so tempting and her curiosity was running wild, but she didn't want her new husband to know that she was snooping. While Keith was in the other room working on a project, DeAnn rolled out the vacuum cleaner and turned it on to create noise to cover her exploring. Then she crawled under the tree and reached to the far corners to find her presents. Before long, her husband wondered why the vacuum cleaner didn't seem to be moving. He came into the room to find his lovely wife, under the tree, peeking into packages.

Sometimes the gift you are giving is so large or cumbersome that it is difficult to wrap. A technique we have often used is to wrap a small box with a clue inside as to where they might find the gift. This is fun when it becomes a treasure hunt complete with clues that lead the recipient through the house and may end in the garage or basement.

Another method of giving a very large gift is to wrap a picture of the item in a very small box. The lightness of this box gives the receiver a moment to wonder if the box contains anything of worth. It surely doesn't rattle or swish as you shake it!

For very small gifts, it is always fun to make them seem larger. Wrap the small gift very carefully and then place it in a larger box, perhaps including another item, then place that box in another and on and on as far as you wish to go. It makes the gift-opening time fun as you all laugh together over the various creative packages and "find" the final treasure.

When you gather the family for the opening of gifts, have a plan as to who will open a gift and when. It is more fun to open gifts if one person at a time opens a gift and all get to watch the facial expressions of the recipient of the gift. You may wish to take turns as you sit in a circle or you may do it by age from the youngest to the oldest. Letting everyone tear into their packages at the same time creates a bit of chaos, and small pieces may be lost in the process. Part of the fun of giving is seeing the other person's delight over a gift.

Darin has decided the best way to keep Peggy from shaking and prodding until she accidentally creates a tear in the wrapping is to use duct tape to secure the wrapping. She knows who the duct-taped gift is from and I think she has given up trying to ferret out what it contains.

Gag gifts are always good for a laugh, if done in good taste and if they are not designed to cause hurt. Our son, Rod, and his father-in-law, Dwain, have had great fun giving a "blunderbar" back and forth. Last Christmas, grandson Kyle was the recipient of this wonderful, bent, rusty bar. Kyle says he may give it to an uncle this year. Hiding behind different types of wrapping and in various containers, it has provided lots of healthy laughs.

Dawn, our daughter-in-law, became the owner of a wall hanging made from soda cans and decided to surprise her mom with the elegant gift. Wrapping the wall hanging in a beautiful box with a pretty ribbon, she gave the gift to her mother. The puzzled look of surprise on Joyce's face was fun for all present to witness. The wall hanging makes its rounds each Christmas, and now Tiffany plans to give it to Auntie Lynelle. The surprise of opening an elegant package and finding the soda can wall hanging has been fun.

When Dick Stenbakken was attending the theological seminary, he acquired a small ceramic frog. The frog was posed, lying on its side, holding its head up with its arm, and had a silly grin on its face. One year Dick wrapped this frog and gave it to his wife, Ardis, for Christmas. A tradition was born. Every Christmas after that, the Frog would show up somewhere, somehow. One was never quite sure who would get the Frog or even who had the Frog and who might be giving it.

When their son, Erik, was in Ponopei as a student missionary, the Frog made his way to the tropics to let Erik know he was still part of the family circle. Daughter, Rikki, was married on New Year's Day. On Christmas Day, the week before, her husband-to-be, Jason, received the Frog. Jason was now a member of the family. Occasionally the Frog will show up as a gift for some other gift-giving event, but it is usually Christmas. No Christmas would be complete without the traditional appearance of the Frog.

Peggy just confessed, "One year I decided to open several of my presents and wrap them up again, so I wouldn't be disappointed when I opened any of them on Christmas Eve. So I did—and I wasn't disappointed—or surprised—on Christmas Eve!"

This year I have found the perfect gift for Peggy—a "music box" that is labeled "Package Shakers Patrol." When the switch is turned on, a siren wails to warn everyone that the package shaker is on the prowl. We will laugh together and enjoy the fun of this gift.

Church groups and other clubs have Christmas parties and exchange gifts. A fun way to facilitate the exchange is for one person to choose a gift. All wait until the gift is opened and the next person has the choice of choosing a wrapped gift or taking the one from the person who just opened his/hers. Each person then goes through the same steps. If a gift is taken from someone, the individual then chooses a wrapped gift or one from someone else. Gag gifts are especially fun to use at these parties.

When her children were little, RuthAnn MacDonald began a practice of wrapping each small gift she gave her children. If it is a pair of socks, pencils, or another small item, she wraps it in its own package. Having small gifts as well as larger ones makes the gift exchange more fun.

"Mother wraps each gift she gives us separately. It may be lip balm, a toothbrush, or video tapes, but they are all wrapped creatively," says April Mundall.

Giving gifts to friends and family should be fun, and there should be an element of surprise and mystery about the gift. With a little thought and creativity this can be accomplished without a lot of effort or expense. Make the family gift exchange fun!

Hanging the Stockings

Children love to hang their stockings on Christmas Eve and eagerly look forward to opening the little gifts on Christmas morning. Stockings of every description are hung from fireplace mantles or, in the absence of a fireplace, on the arms of chairs and couches, on hooks fastened to the wall, or in other creative spots.

Because of the lack of fresh fruit in years gone by, children often received the special treat of a fresh orange or some other fruit in their stocking. Hard candies, nuts, and other goodies were also included as parents filled their children's stockings. Whistles, horns, and other little toys peeked out of the tops of each stocking.

My husband still likes to add these items as he fills the stockings. Several years ago the children persuaded him that the hard candies should either be wrapped in plastic or not be put in their stockings. They didn't find the lint that clung to the sticky candy very appetizing. The tradition of fruit, candy, and nuts continues at our house.

"One year Rod, Judy and I decided that we should do stockings for our parents," Peggy writes about a special memory. "I remember we spent much time deciding what should go in their stockings. Then we had to decide who was going to get up early in the morning and fill them and who was going to sneak the stockings out of their dresser drawers. Now it is a tradition that Judy and only Judy gets to buy the after-shave lotion for Dad's stocking."

The stockings we now hang are of calico fabrics made according to a pattern in a magazine that intrigued Judy when she was very young. She thought they would be fun to have and to use, so together we planned and made them. The ones for the ladies are in traditional Christmas colors and have various designs and decorations. The men's stockings are of blue denim and made to resemble a cowboy boot.

Our daughter-in-law, Dawn, made beautiful crewel embroidered stockings for her family to use at Christmas. Each one has its own Christmas scene depicted on the front. She hangs them from the mantle as part of her Christmas decorations and on Christmas Eve they are filled, ready to be opened on Christmas morning.

Lois Bray started a tradition of brown paper bags. Each Christmas morning, her children found a brown paper bag with their "stocking" gifts. Their daughter, Laura, still asks, "Where are the brown bags?" The tradition means home is still there and important, even though she is now living miles away from Mom and Dad.

The opening of the Christmas stocking on Christmas morning is a special part of Christmas to those who have grown up with this tradition. Inexpensive, simple, and yet fun, Christmas stockings are one of the memories families cherish.

Christmas is for kids . . .

"I remember when I was in Kindergarten, I wanted a doll that felt like a real baby. That was probably all I wanted that Christmas. And when Christmas came I had lots of presents that day, including the doll I wanted so much. I had a new baby brother named Max, and since I couldn't carry Max around all the time, I pretended that Cassey was a real baby. I could take care of her all the time.

"I still have that doll, but I don't play with it a lot anymore. Every year, when it's time for the Christmas play, she's usually baby Jesus, so she's still special."

–Courtney Tasche, Fourth Grade

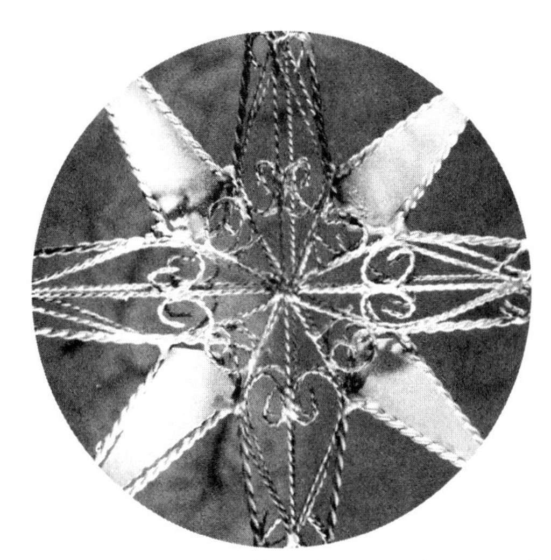

"The tree may be as tall and its branches as wide as shall best suit the occasion; but let its boughs be laden with the golden and silver fruit of your beneficence, and present this to Him as your Christmas gift. Let your donations be sanctified by prayer"

(The Adventist Home, p. 482).

Christmas in God's House

Praising God for the gift of His Son brings a special share of joy to our hearts. Our church services during the holiday season can provide a way to share that joy with many others. We can also follow the example of the wise men and bring our gifts to Him.

Different churches choose to decorate in various ways. Green wreaths with ribbon bows are often seen on the doors entering into the church. Grapevine wreaths hung at the front of the church on either side of the rostrum lift your spirits as you look at the reminder of the season. Some churches display trees that are decorated very simply and elegantly, and others have more decorations. All congregations express their individuality as they prepare their sanctuary for Christmas.

A beautiful tradition in some churches is to have the congregation present their offerings by placing them on the Christmas tree. With the tree placed at the front of the church, those present come forward while Christmas carols are played or sung and place their offering on and among the branches. The offerings of bills are tucked between the branches and a basket beneath the tree is available to receive coins.

To make giving a pleasant experience for the children, Jeanette Davidson prepared small bags made of felt in the shape of stars and stockings in which the children placed their offerings. After putting their offerings in these bags, they hung them on the tree at the front of the church. Some teachers help the children make a paper chain of dollar bills, clipped together with paper clips. The children then place this garland on the tree. After the service the "decorations" are removed and the money given to missions. All are reminded of the privilege we have of returning to the Master just a little of what He has given us.

Other churches choose to make the season special by having programs with children portraying the story of the birth of Jesus. With song and verse they retell the story of the shepherds on the hillside listening to the angels tell them to go and find the Baby Jesus. Dressed in costumes similar to the culture of the area around Bethlehem in the time of Jesus, the children portray the scene of Mary and Joseph by the manger cradling Baby Jesus.

Pastors often draw upon their story-telling talents and make the story come alive as they recount the evening of Jesus' birth. Interspersed with appropriate Christmas songs, this service touches hearts with the wonder of this wonderful gift that was given to us and for us.

Communities frequently form a community choir and give concerts before Christmas. Simple presentations are often the most moving and beautiful. The different churches in our community have formed such a choir and presented an evening of carols. Singing the familiar carols without props and other staging allowed the audience to meditate on the message of the songs. Other churches present cantatas and plays to celebrate the birthday of our Lord. Christmas is an opportune time to join with other Christian faiths in sharing the story of the awe-inspiring birth that binds us together.

Ardis shares this story from the years her husband Dick Stenbakken was a chaplain in the U. S. Army.

"During the twenty-four years of service one of the family traditions was that of attending Christmas Eve services. Each Army post always had a Christmas Eve service, usually in the main post chapel. It was attended by almost all of the higher ranking officers and almost everyone who ever attended the chapel services. The officers partaking, usually the commanding general and others, including Dick, wore their dress blue uniforms, which always looked so sharp. The chapels were inevitably nicely decorated and had the best music the post had to offer. The services were always quite short and simple but moving and concluded with the lighting of candles. When our children were small, they loved to collect all the burnt candles after the service. We had enough candles all year for any possible need."

A meaningful Christmas for Candy Seltman was one shared with friends at their church:

"Family traditions are simply the joy of shared experiences. The preparation and excitement of the school Christmas programs, going to the Presbyterian church with my aunt and watching my friends do their church program was one of these experiences. We all enjoyed the Christmas candy, peanuts, oranges, and apples from the brown paper bags they gave to all the children after the performance. It was an important part of my childhood holiday celebration."

The Leonard and Lorraine Payne family had a tradition of caroling during the Christmas holidays when their children were young. Lorraine made capes for each of the children, of white oil cloth decorated with a big red bow, to keep them dry in the wet winter weather of Portland, Oregon. The kids and Lorraine would sing as they went from door to door and Leonard visited with the people in the homes as they opened their door and listened to the music. He explained this was their family project to raise money for mission work and the people gave generously.

Janis Vance wrote that her family had a similar tradition. Their church members would dress warmly and go through the neighborhood singing for the neighbors and friends.

"People would open their doors to listen to us sing and offered candy and hot apple cider. Their homes would be cozy and warm, and we enjoyed singing. We also accepted gifts of money to be used for charity work. When we met back at the church and shared how nice the people were to us, I knew that even as a child, I was part of a very special evening. A community of people, young and old, was willing to give up warm cozy nights at home to work together for a bigger purpose. Now, as an adult, I realize how we were blessed as we sang for others."

A beautiful timeless tradition still carried on in some churches is the giving of Christmas treats to the children after the evening program. These churches make a special effort to invite those children who may not have a Christmas celebration in their homes. It provides a comfortable opportunity to give a gift to the children in a manner that does not make them feel like they are the recipients of charity.

Commemorating Christmas with our church family is an important tradition for many families. It provides us an opportunity to gather as a family to rejoice and praise God for this blessed season.

✦ ✦

THE FAITH OF A CHILD

"One year in California when I was in Kindergarten, it started snowing. Now that was a very special thing for California.

"Christmas was not very far away and that Christmas was scary. My baby cousin stopped breathing. I went in a corner and prayed to Jesus. I said, 'Dear Jesus, please help my cousin. Amen.' Just as I said Amen, he started to breathe again! Then I said, 'Thank You, Jesus, for helping baby Anthony.' And the rest of the night was Christmas delight."

–Chris Nelson, Third Grade

Christmas is for kids . . .

"My family watches the Christmas Story on video on Christmas Eve."

—*Shawn Sweningson, First Grade*

Christmas is a time of coziness and family togetherness.

A Family Evening

Christmas Eve finds families gathered around a lighted tree, often with candles and oil lamps providing light to read and share Christmas stories, family programs, and gifts. Although many different stories are shared, traditionally the story recorded in Luke 2 is the first one read.

Eddie Heinrich tells of Christmas Eve at his home:

"One of the things I remember most about Christmas—growing up—was that we opened our presents on Christmas Eve. However, it happened only after my mother, who loved to read, read us the complete unabridged version of the book, 'The Other Wise Man.' It tells the story of the fourth Wise Man, who is always a little late in his attempt to find Jesus, so instead of giving his gifts to Jesus he finds himself using the gifts he brought for Jesus to help people who were in desperate straits. It was great to lie on the floor eating oranges, cracking walnuts, and listening to Dad snore while Mom read us the entire book.

"Occasionally she would stop reading, and my Dad would wake up and insist that he had not been asleep and that she should continue to read. If she quizzed him on what was happening in the story, he would tell her, and either she always stopped in the same place or he was sleeping with one ear open. He almost always got it right."

Fifth grader Kayla Haugen tells of Christmas Eve at their home:

"I think Christmas is all about sharing. Every year my Mom or Dad reads the story about Mary and Joseph traveling to Bethlehem to be counted and when Baby Jesus was born. We eat supper, then open our presents. Sometimes we watch a Christmas movie."

April Mundall recalls reading the Christmas stories her mother has collected through the years. Her favorite is "No Man Need Walk Alone," about Esau Tinker and his willingness to share his wooden leg with someone who did not have one.

Our family enjoys telling stories of past Christmases and the family members who have shared them with us. There is a warm and comfortable feeling as we share memories. The stories are a mixture of funny, poignant, sad, and joyful times. By talking together, we keep family history and traditions alive.

"Hearing the sleigh bells announcing it was Christmas Eve and time to read the Christmas story from Luke and sing Christmas carols around the old pump organ, while mother played, made it really seem like Christmas," remembers Candy Seltman.

Leonard and Lorraine Payne and their family gathered together with uncles, aunts, and cousins on Christmas Eve. Those present all contributed to an impromptu program. Songs, pantomimes, poems, carols, and other presentations made for an enjoyable evening prior to gift-opening time.

Ruth Johnson also remembers:

"Christmas Eve was strictly for just the family when I was a child. We usually had lutefisk and lefsa for supper. After the dishes were done everyone gathered in the living room. Some of the children had a recitation or song before the gifts were opened. When finally the gifts were opened, we played games and enjoyed the specially made snacks, nuts, and candy. We usually didn't have much candy in those days. We lived twenty miles from town and had no car as yet."

Our son-in-law, Darin Kelstrom, writes the following:

"Growing up on a dairy farm, as children, my sister and I had to develop some patience on Christmas Eve. Before the presents could be opened, all the animals had to be fed and the cows in the barn milked.

"While this was happening, my sister and I would look under the tree and see all the gifts that were tagged to us and, of course, shake them just a little. To pass the time we would listen to the story of Christ's birth on the Bible Story records.

"We were really attentive to the time as it seemed like forever before Dad came in from the barn. We would keep looking out the window and see how many lights were still on in the barn. One by one they would go out till finally there were no more lights on in the barn and the only ones left were the lights in the milk house as Dad was finishing up. The excitement for us was building so much that when Dad came in we met him at the back door and told him to hurry and get ready because we couldn't wait any longer. Dad would smile and of course he would not hurry any faster than necessary in order to give us a 'bad time.' Finally everyone was ready and the package opening began.

"On Christmas Eve, humans were not the only ones that got extra, for you see all the animals got a little extra hay and a little extra formula for they helped us have a good Christmas."

Opening gifts on Christmas Eve is a tradition many families share. Other families choose to open their gifts on Christmas morning. Our family remembers Kyle's first Christmas Eve when he was a little more than ten months old. How careful he was to just rip a little piece of the paper off and then pick it up and put it in the bag where we were putting the torn wrapping paper. It took a long time to open a package when he went little piece by little piece. Now he just rips into them like all kids.

Some memories are so precious and meaningful for different reasons. Billie Jean Knight tells of the Christmas they traveled from Loma Linda, California to San Felipe in Baja California, Mexico.

"It was Christmas 1959 when three adults and four children along with their sleeping bags made this trip in a VW bug. Someone had previously driven down with a fourteen-foot travel trailer with supplies. The family slept under the stars in a two-walled 'cabana' with a cement floor. I remember that Christmas Eve we took a walk on the beach and saw the tide pools but chose not to explore them in the dark. I was able to watch the stars throughout the night whenever I awoke. I watched the constellation, Orion, go from east to west overnight.

Christmas spent with family even though we had to travel was the best way to celebrate the season."

Evie VandeVere contributed the following story about an unusual but meaningful Christmas Eve spent with family. She titled it:

A Missouri Christmas

"Where's Davy?" I asked, upon entering Aunt Winifred's kitchen, from which emanated the most tantalizing smells of a vegetarian holiday roast (made from Grandma Van's hand-washed gluten!) mingled with the sweet smell of cinnamon rolls and pumpkin pies. Taking a break from reading, I had wandered through the adjoining dining room where David's siblings, Rhonda, Robbie, and Jodi were playing PROBE with their Grandpa Van. Davy's absence was noticeable since he almost always "played with Grandpa" during these games.

"He's out in the pasture with Uncle Isom gathering wood for our bonfire tonight." replied Grandma Van.

"A bonfire? On Christmas Eve?" I questioned.

"Yes," said Aunt Winifred, "it's so warm outside, we decided it would be fun to have a picnic supper with a bonfire out in the pasture on the hill tonight."

"A Christmas Eve birthday picnic supper." I was thinking of our youngest daughter who made her debut into the family on Christmas Eve. "What a unique celebration for Jodi."

Sure enough, darkness found six adults and four children hiking, our arms full of food and blankets, as well as coat hangers for roasting marshmallows. Flashlights illuminated the crooked path out to the pasture. We must have made quite a sight, more like shepherds than wise men, I thought.

It was not hard to find the site of our picnic, for suddenly up ahead to the right of the path we saw a huge mound of dead branches, twigs, and some wood. A scrape of a match, a touch of the small flame to the kindling, and fiery tongues quickly reached out and upward, shedding a broad circle of light in front of us.

We stood around the fire, mesmerized by the dancing flames. It didn't take long to cover the ground with blankets and a tablecloth. Aunt Winifred and Grandma Van sat down on a corner of the blanket and began to make sandwiches for the rest of us. Their sixty and seventy-year old agility amazed me as I shifted around, seeking a comfortable position.

We ate while watching the bonfire, listening to its comfortable, crackling sound, quietly talking and laughing as the children hurriedly ate their sandwiches in anticipation of roasting marshmallows for their dessert.

Perched as we were on such steep ground, the hill became a pillow when, after eating, I laid back on my blanket to gaze at the stars that seemed so close and touchable. Far up among the sparkling constellations, I saw the blinking lights of an airplane. I wondered if they could see our bonfire.

Pushing myself up to a sitting position I gazed at the adults sitting and talking quietly and at our children contentedly munching on their burnt, sticky marshmallows. My thoughts drifted to another scene, another hillside and another bonfire surrounded by shepherds who probably were talking or maybe sleeping on just such a night as this. How startled they must have been as the glory of the Lord made daylight of their night with the sudden appearance of the angel. Fear must have been so evident in their faces, for the angel's first words were, "Do not be afraid." And then the reason. "I bring you good news of great joy that will be for all the people. Today in the town of David a Savior has been born to you; He is Christ the Lord."

Handel's music rang in my ears as I imagined being

there to hear that glorious music as the angels praised God and sang, "Glory to God in the highest, and on earth peace and good will to all men."

Looking up at the sky, I could still see the lights of the plane. Silently I wished all of its passengers a "Merry Christmas" and prayed for them a safe journey as it disappeared into the starry darkness that memorable Christmas Eve on a Missouri hillside.

Quiet evenings spent with the family, whether gathered in one room enjoying the Christmas decorations, lights, and stories, or on a Missouri hillside, all make cherished memories come alive and create new memories. Warm, cozy moments that will make us all want to "come home for Christmas" in the years ahead, even if only in our memories.

CHRISTMAS IS FOR KIDS . . .

"My favorite parts of Christmas are the food, Christmas carols, and traditions. All of those things have special meaning to me. The food: My grandma prepares one of the best Christmas dinners ever! Christmas carols: I love to sing! Right after dinner we all gather around the piano and sing Christmas carols. Then last, but not least, tradition: Every year after dinner and singing my grandma opens her presents first because it's her birthday. Then we open presents from youngest to oldest. I am so glad that my family does these traditions that make Christmas special."

–Jason Peck, Sixth Grade

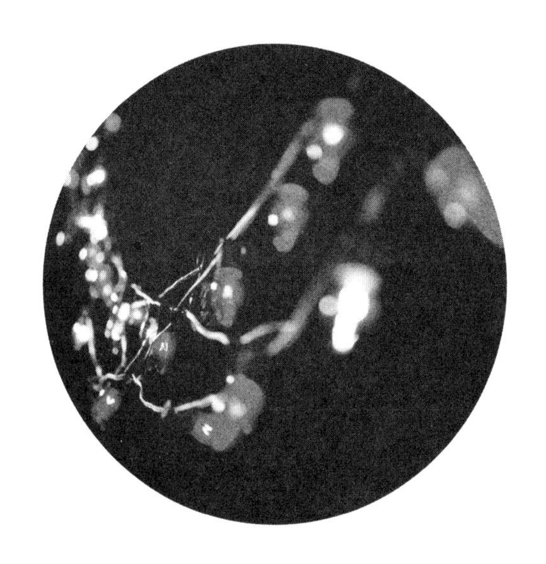

Years cannot erase the cherished memories of friends and family.

Welcome to Our Home!

After decorating our homes for the season, it is always fun to invite our family and friends to share our home and enliven it with good conversation and tasty food. Families have various ways of opening their homes to others. Some open their homes to members of the community during a Christmas Open House Tour to raise money for a charitable organization, others prefer to have family and friends share their homes.

Our family has traditionally celebrated each Christmas by inviting aunts, uncles, and others who may not have family with them at Christmas time and would be alone. This custom has brightened our celebrations and given us many memories.

One Christmas there were going to be only four of

us for Christmas dinner. It just didn't seem right to be so few. Christmas morning I remembered that our neighbors, Theresa and Ernie Vatthauer and their daughter, Kim, were also going to be alone for dinner. I called Theresa and asked if they would think of putting their dinner on hold and come and join us. They were happy to do this, and we remember this as a "spur of the moment" celebration that brought joy to our home.

As I visited with Becky Christensen Carlisle, I heard about the beautiful tradition they have of sharing their home during the Christmas season. Becky is a music teacher and plans and gives programs for the school and the church each year. In addition to these activities, she and her husband, Maurice (now deceased), established the tradition of a Christmas Open House for their friends, neighbors, and family. This is a tradition that has continued for more than twenty years.

Kristen, her daughter, wrote this account of their open house:

"Many families celebrate the holidays with passed-down traditions. The Carlisle family Christmas is filled with many traditions. The most celebrated and anticipated is the open house. It fills much of our time as we cook, clean, and prepare for the party that our Christmas holiday is based around. Finally the long-awaited time arrives.

"Members of our church family, neighbors, and friends gather together around the snack table to munch on the feast of homemade cookies and candies. If they are not pondering over which cookies to fill themselves with, they are in the living room surrounding the grand piano, singing carols. A fiddler often joins with the singing, adding a sense of country living to the atmosphere. When they tire of singing, the guests wend their way to the family room where Bing Crosby is heard singing 'White Christmas' on the stereo. Here punch is served, and everyone is trying to make sure they say 'hello' to all of their friends. The women work in shifts to keep the table full of goodies.

"Parents show off their children and send them to the movie room to enjoy a Christmas film. Chatting without interruption from their children, the parents enjoy the opportunity to fellowship with other adults. Warmth fills the house, whether it be from the burning fire or from the many bodies filling the house at one time. Laughter and chitchat fill the air, leaving no room for gloom. It is a time to relax and see friends and family. Stories and pictures of children and grandchildren are exchanged.

"When the children's heads start to nod in sleep and the evening comes to a close, the women stand in the kitchen to give Mom a hug and ask for their favorite cookie recipe. The men say their good-byes and try to get their wives to leave their friends so they can go home and put the children to bed.

"After the last of our guests have left, we head off to bed to rest. Leaving the 'cleanup' for the morning, we snuggle into bed with warm memories and thankful hearts for the love of friends and family."

Christmas, 1997, was drawing near, and once again the Carlisle family was prepared for their annual open house. Maurice became ill and died very unexpectedly, leaving a family mourning for a beloved husband and father. The family made the decision to go ahead with the open house, and it became a time of comfort and brought healing to their hearts as their friends and family came to express their love and sympathy. Becky said, "It was so good to have people around us on that day, and, after all, it's a Carlisle Tradition!"

As Becky shared this heart-touching story, it reinforced my belief that traditions are important to a family. They not only carry us through the good times but also through the sad times.

Our friends, Pauline and Bill Purath, were blessed with a new daughter-in-law that they wanted to introduce to their family, friends, and community. Since the wedding had taken place in England and none of us were able to attend, we were thrilled to be invited to a Christmas Open House at their home to once again see Doug and meet his lovely bride, Donna. The holidays are a time when families come from far and near and it is a good time for all to visit and renew friendships. Their Christmas Open House in honor of Doug and Donna provided us with that opportunity.

The first year we were married, I joined a Home Study Group in our neighborhood. It gave me occasions to meet my new neighbors and get to know them as individuals. At Christmas we invited our husbands to a "Christmas Potluck." This doubled the size of our usual group and we needed a little extra room to provide tables with places for everyone to sit. For several years, we met in our basement where we put up tables and chairs and decorated appropriately. It was a joy to plan for this gathering and then to enjoy the time of fellowship and friendship. This potluck has become an annual event.

The tables are covered with red, white, and green tablecloths and have a simple centerpiece on each one. Serving buffet style makes the entertaining easy and relaxed. Exchanging gifts with our secret sisters and a Christmas reading are a part of the party.

Some years while the tables are still all set up, we have gathered for one day to sew pajamas for children in families where Christmas gifts may not be so plentiful. Lucille Weiss has been the organizer for this event. Going to the County Social Service, we have been given information about boys and girls, their sizes and their ages, so we could make appropriate garments for them. The sewing "bees" gave us another opportunity to enjoy each other and to deepen our friendships. Other years we have taken a collection and used the money to buy gifts for children in homes for the disabled. These activities have made our Christmases together blessed.

Rilda Pengra writes:

"Each Christmas with our Christian mother was memorable. However, it isn't difficult to remember probably one of the most memorable Christmases that I have ever experienced. It went beyond usual Christmas traditions that a family carries over from one year to the next. Our mother was widowed when her son was sixteen months old, and her twin daughters were eight days old. In 1938, this left her with little more than the love and moral support of her family but greater than all, the love of Jesus.

"Having grown up in a loving Christian family, Mother continued her belief and faith in God throughout her life. She was a devoted daughter to her parents and wanted to spend as many holidays with them as possible. Sometimes this created a problem as Mother did have to go to work when we started school.

"But each Christmas, she would ask for the holiday off so we could go to Grandma's and Grandpa's. There was nothing that brought the love of the season closer to us than crawling up on our grandparents' laps and feeling their love as they received our hugs and affection. So the three of us children felt we had a 'double dose' of love from our grandparents and Mother.

"Our mother never failed to show this love to others. One Christmas, for some reason, we did not go to our grandparents. Christmas morning we went to church where we met a former pastor who had come to visit. He had brought guests from his church to our church in Hot Springs, South Dakota for this Christmas Sabbath.

"The pastor and his wife were invited to some friends' for Christmas dinner after church. I don't remember why their guests did not go with them to this home, but the visiting pastor asked our mother if she would mind taking these guests home with us for dinner. Mother, being the loving and wonderfully caring person that she was, was only too happy to oblige. So to our home we all went for our special Christmas dinner.

"The three of 'us kids' can remember to this day what our menu was on that special Christmas Sabbath when we entertained our new friends. The menu varied little from week to week due to the limited budget. Our Native American friends enjoyed the Swiss steak, potatoes, baked beans, homemade rolls, lime Jell-O with cottage cheese, crushed pineapple and mayonnaise, and for dessert, Mother's delicious chocolate cake. Christmas time was special and we usually had more fresh fruit and different nuts as well.

"So we shared our Christmas that year with friends of our former pastor and his wife. It was a Christmas that shall always be imbedded in our memories because, unlike when Jesus was born and there was no room in the inn, our Mother always had room for everyone and she cared not their color, status, origin, or anything else. She simply loved people and shared her love that special day with friends whom we had never met before. To me that was one of the greatest Christmases I have ever known. It was Mother's tradition to always have room in her 'Inn' for everyone and we were reminded of this that day."

Francis and Bill Wilson held an open house for their church members when they had just moved to a new church district. They had moved in October and were just nicely settled in time to have everyone over. One of their members arrived early with a beautiful centerpiece for the table—which was just the finishing touch for their preparations. Their cookies and hot and cold beverages made the evening festive.

Darrell and I have had many a chuckle over the fact that we drove three hundred miles one way to attend a Christmas Open House at Dennis and Ann Carlson's home and drove back the three hundred miles the next day. It was fun and well worth the time spent traveling to and from their house. (Of course we also did manage an overnight visit with our daughter and son-in-law.)

As we were eating supper, I noticed Dennis and a friend kept going outdoors and wondered where they were going and what they were doing. Then came the realization that they were going to the house across the street to bring back casserole dishes that were being kept warm in the neighbor's oven. The neighbors were enjoying serving their friends as keepers of the ovens.

After the delicious supper we were entertained with an evening of Christmas musical numbers by the Maplewood Academy musical group who had been invited to the supper and to sing for us.

Their beautiful Christmas decorations, the warm fellowship, the music, and the good food made the evening a pleasure. As we admired the tree and its ornaments, Ann shared the stories behind many of the handmade ones and those they had received as gifts. Then she made me feel very special by removing one of the ornaments she had made and giving it to me. It was an evening to be stored in memory and worthy of the drive.

Holiday entertaining can be small dinner parties, teas, an evening of visiting with dessert served, or having friends drop over for a few minutes. Homes are blessed when we share them with others, especially at Christmas time.

Christmas is for kids . . .

"Christmas means Jesus was born, and pretty decorations."

–Olivia Edelbach, First Grade

Families who have strong traditions are healthy families.

Building New Family Traditions

Those who have grown up in families without Christmas traditions have to choose to build their own. By giving a little thought to what your family values are and what you like to do together, developing traditions becomes fun and easy. Traditions are what you as a family want them to be. Runette Litzenberger has written so very well about their family's building of traditions. I felt it is a good example of "how to" start traditions within a family, so I am including it just as she has written it.

Litzenberger Family Traditions

My husband and I were married the last day of November 1975 and I became Mom to a four-and-a-half year-old boy. Christmas needed no traditions that year. We were settling in as a new family and were just thankful we had each other.

The following Christmas our house was in a tizzy because we had shipped our goods to the mission field and sold most of what we hadn't shipped. No traditions were begun that year, either.

Our third Christmas as a family was spent in Jakarta, Indonesia and we just enjoyed the local culture and people around us.

Our fourth Christmas found us living on the island of Guam, with a seven-month-old daughter added to our family. We were beginning to hear family life experts talk about the importance of traditions that families plan together and children look forward to. So we started giving thought to what kind of Christmastime activities we would like to make traditions in our home. Our goal was to choose mostly those activities that were not only fun and enjoyable, but meaningful and would provide learning experiences as well.

The first idea we developed into a tradition began while we lived on Guam, where our son celebrated his seventh, eighth and ninth birthdays, and where our two daughters were born. We learned many Guamanians would set up a manger in their homes for Christmas, rather than a Christmas tree (evergreens are not indigenous to Guam!). In our home, we decided we would decorate our (artificial) Christmas tree and we would set up a manger next to the tree. The manger was a box stuffed with a pillow and covered with a sheet, which flowed out over the box and onto the floor. Baby Jesus was a baby doll I had received for my tenth birthday. It was swaddled in a receiving blanket.

This tradition grew through the ensuing years to include the three children dressing up like Mary, Joseph and a shepherd, while Dad read the Christmas story from the Bible on Christmas morning. The children took turns playing each of the three roles. Of course, whoever played Mary got to hold Baby Jesus during the story.

Also from the time we put the Christmas tree up and set out the manger until we put them both away, each evening one of the children would get to hold Baby Jesus during family worship. It was surprising that something that simple was always greatly anticipated and Baby Jesus was always held very reverently and lovingly. When worship was over, Baby Jesus was carefully laid back in the manger until the next evening.

Wanting to encourage our children to enjoy giving more than receiving, and to see in a tangible way whether we, as a family, were doing more receiving or more giving, we began placing gifts for our family under the tree and gifts we were giving to people outside our family around the manger. We would talk about where the most gifts were located and where Jesus would like most of the gifts to be.

As this new tradition progressed year after year, we would hear comments like, "Mommy, we have too many presents under the tree. We need to give more to other people so we'll have more around the manger." Or, "We have lots of presents around the manger. Jesus is happy."

As the children got older, we thought they would lose interest in the manger being set up and intentionally would not set it up to see what would happen. For several years, the question always came: "Where is the manger? When will we set it up?" At which time, we would place the manger in its familiar location.

Many photographs of the children portraying Mary, Joseph, the shepherd and with the doll representing Baby Jesus are in our family albums bring back happy memories whenever we look at them.

Secret Angels is another tradition our family enjoyed. For several years the children looked forward to being a "secret angel" to another family member. We would put each name on a slip of paper, fold the papers and place them in a basket. Then we would each draw a name out and we would be the "secret angel" to that person during the several weeks from Thanksgiving to Christmas. We would look for ways to do nice things for "our" person, but try to do them in such a way that "our" person wouldn't know who did them.

For instance, "our" person may rush out to school and leave an unmade bed or leave their bedroom untidy. The "secret angel" might make the bed and straighten the room. It was fun for all of us as we looked for ways to do nice things for each other in secret. (It was especially fun for Mom to watch Dad thinking up "special" things he could do for one of his children in secret!) On Christmas day we would find out who had been our "secret angel."

Another tradition our children enjoyed for many years was that of an Advent calendar. We would always look for a very colorful, festive-looking calendar, preferably one with a religious theme, which included Scripture references. We would keep the calendar on the kitchen table or held by magnets on the refrigerator door. Every morning after breakfast, we would open another door on the calendar. I was sad when the children all reached the age when the Advent calendar was no longer a tradition that they looked forward to.

Some traditions are limited by age and interest of the children, as with the Advent calendar, but others never seem to be outgrown. We have found this to be true of two of our traditions: yearly tree ornaments and our immediate family Christmas Eve Party.

While we lived in Guam, we decided it would be special to give each of our children a new tree ornament every Christmas and when they left home, they would have their ornament collection for their own tree. So, each year when we are ready to decorate our tree, we talk about how old the child was when he or she received a particular ornament, where we lived at that time and anything else they might remember about Christmas at that time of their lives.

When I was a stay-at-home mom, I made the ornaments, but as the children got older and I began working outside our home, I haven't always had the time to make ornaments, so we have purchased ornaments we felt would be special to each child. When our son married several years ago, we gave him his ornaments and he indicated how special it was to have them for the first Christmas tree in his own home.

Christmas is an exciting time for children and they are always anxious to know what is in the packages. We thought we could spread out the fun if we didn't open everything all at one time. So we began a tradition of opening gifts in the stockings on Christmas Eve and gifts from under the tree on Christmas morning. After we were married, I crocheted a large stocking for our son, and as the girls were born, I crocheted them each a large stocking. It was always such fun to fill them with surprises when the children were little. (It is still fun to find surprises for the stocking, but we have also discovered that as the children have become young adults, the surprises seem to get more costly!)

Every Christmas Eve for the beginning of our family Christmas Party, we have the "children" sit near each other (for the sake of picture taking) and take turns removing a gift from their stocking and opening it.

After the stocking gifts are opened, we have a supper buffet set out on a table nicely decorated for Christmas. Usually it is a light supper including Christmas "goodies"—nuts, cookies, candies, etc.—as well as peppermint ice cream and eggnog. (The last several years we have been leaving off the eggnog for health reasons and actually eating less and less of the "goodies.") We fill our plates and gather in front of the television to watch the video "White

Christmas," a musical that our whole family enjoys and looks forward to viewing every Christmas Eve.

The Christmas Eve Party has become our longest-standing tradition. In fact, when our son left home and married he told us he had purchased the video "White Christmas" and he and his wife would be having a family Christmas Eve Party the way he knew we would be doing at home.

As I am writing this, the memories are all coming back and I am feeling a bit nostalgic. Our son is twenty-eight and has been away from home and able to spend only one Christmas with us in the last several years. Our two daughters are college students living at home. But we know we won't have them with us many more years.

Christmas time is still enjoyable. However, it is a different kind of joy than when our children were smaller. We all still look forward to our family Christmas Eve Party, but the Advent calendar and holding Baby Jesus during evening family worship time are gone forever. Yet, the memories are there, not only in Mom's and Dad's minds, but in the minds of our grown children as well. I know, because they still talk about them. That is what traditions are all about, to give a feeling of security, a sense of family and a knowledge that each one is surrounded by love. Not only family love, but most important, God's love.

To illustrate how impressed a child can be by family traditions, I want to share with you the following composition written by our youngest daughter for a school assignment when she was in the fifth grade.

Christmas Eve at Our House
by Stacy A. Litzenberger

In the driving cold of winter
I sit warm and cozy,
My family near me,

The moon shining on the snow.
Mother is sitting in her housecoat;
Father is in his chair.
Grandma is sitting comfortably by Grandpa.
Brian is sprawled across the floor;
Amy is sitting on the sofa.
All of us watch the movie together.
We enjoy the taste of fresh cookies,
Salty nuts, soft sweet breads,
Sweet punch and eggnog.
Now it is time to open our stockings
Brian first, then Amy, then me.
Pictures are being taken.
The house is warm and loving.
Then we go rushing to bed,
Shutting our eyes tight,
For Christmas is almost here.

I want to thank Runette for sharing how a family, who perhaps does not have a heritage of traditions, can begin their own and make them meaningful and fun.

Christmas is for kids . . .

"Christmas is a time to celebrate the time God's son was born, and for families to get together to exchange gifts. My favorite part of Christmas is the great food my grandma fixes for our big family. Then like all kids I like opening presents just as much. One of the two best presents I have received through the years was a Sony Playstation that I received from my mom and dad. I also like the telescope I received from my grandma and grandpa."

–Joshua Fleming, Eighth Grade

Food and the traditions involved in preparing it are an integral part of Christmas.

Christmas Across the Seas

We who live in the "New World" have a heritage that is the most unique in the world. With the exception of the Native Americans, nearly every one of us finds our heritage in lands across the oceans. Because of our diverse backgrounds, we have blended the traditions brought with our families as they immigrated to the Americas. We have chosen the foods that appeal to our palates and made them a part of our family gatherings. Thus, the foods for our Christmas dinners and other special dishes have their beginnings in other cultures.

Christmas in our busy world has become condensed to Christmas Eve and Christmas Day. It was not always so. In the Early Church, there were twenty-four days of Advent when people thought daily of the first Christmas and came together and worshiped our Savior. After Christmas Day there yet remained the twelve days of Christmas ending with Epiphany on January 6, commemorating the visit of the wise men.

In many areas of the world, one gift is given on each of the twelve days of Christmas. On January 6 more than one gift is given. Our friend Katie told of celebrating on the sixth of January in her home in Kiev, Ukraine of the former Soviet Union. One of my friends celebrates Epiphany by having family and friends over. She lights all of her Christmas candles and together they enjoy the remaining Christmas goodies.

Canada is a vast country with traditions varying from one end to the other. In Nova Scotia, old carols are sung at home and in church. In Newfoundland, the fishermen give their daily catch to the church during Christmas week so it can be sold to raise money for the work of the church. In Vancouver, on the western end of Canada, the harbor area is illuminated with lights. Montreal holds Christmas masses in their beautiful cathedrals. The many ethnic groups remember their heritage and follow customs and traditions from their homelands.

In Russia, Grandfather Frost, accompanied by his granddaughter, is the gift giver. The tree and gift giving have been done at New Year's time. The Orthodox Christmas is in January. In pre-Revolution Russia, the members of the Russian Orthodox Church would fast until after church services on Christmas Eve. More attention is given to December 25 these last few years with more of the traditional decorations again being used.

Our friends south of the border have the Hispanic tradition of "Las Posadas" where children portray the night of Jesus' birth. Each child plays a different part as they go through the neighborhood seeking for a place for the Christ Child to be born. "Posada" means a place to rest for the night. They too continue Christmas with twelve more days and on January 6 the procession of the Three Kings is held and children receive gifts the kings left for them during the night.

Scandinavian traditions are still followed by those of this ancestry. The Sheaf of Grain or the Bird's Christmas Tree is a custom from that area of the world. A sheaf of grain is tied to a pole and placed in the yard for the birds to enjoy a Christmas repast. Including the animals in Christmas by giving them a special treat is a custom followed as a "Thank you" to the animals for providing for them. Farmers love their animals and treat them well. From Sweden we have the lovely tradition of Santa Lucia. In the wee hours of December 13, young girls dressed in white robes with wreaths of lighted candles on their heads, serve pastry and coffee to the parents while they are in bed. Special buns are made with an "X" on them to symbolize Christ.

Another Scandinavian tradition is rice pudding with a hidden almond. Whoever receives the hidden almond in Norway is given a treat. In Sweden the finder of the almond is destined to be married within a year. A Finnish custom is to visit the steam bath before Christmas Eve, to get thoroughly clean before the holiday. Finns also sprinkle straw around the tree and sometimes on the dinner table to remind themselves of the humble birth of Jesus.

From England comes the tradition of sending Christmas cards. The cards typically depicted families enjoying the holiday and acts of charity, so important to the Victorian Christmas spirit. In America, the Christmas card was made popular by the cards produced in 1875 by Louis Prang from his Roxbury, Massachusetts shop. His cards featured Nativity scenes, family gatherings, nature scenes, and much later, Santa.

Also from England comes the tradition of Boxing Day. In England, it was customary for churches to parcel out the contents of their alms boxes to the poor on the first workday after Christmas. Out of this custom grew the tradition of employers and those who are blessed with more of this world's goods to share with those in need. Today ordinary families pack boxes of Christmas treats to give to the poor.

In Greece, a special bread is made called Christopsomo or Christ Bread. This bread is usually decorated with a symbol that depicts the family's occupation. Some traditions call for giving the first piece of the loaf to a beggar. A second bread is baked for the animals.

The Christmas seal which in America is used to raise funds for lung diseases originated in Denmark. Einar Holboell felt there should be a special stamp to benefit those who suffered from tuberculosis. The first seal was printed in 1904 with a picture of Queen Louise of Denmark. Emily Bissell of the Red Cross initiated the idea of using a seal to raise funds to keep a tuberculosis treatment center open. School children sold Christmas seals in an effort to promote the eradication of the disease.

The very first Christmas postage stamps were printed in Canada in 1898. The United States did not adopt this custom until 1962. Now we wouldn't think of sending our Christmas greetings without using a special Christmas stamp. Through the years many designs have been used.

In 1224, St. Francis of Assisi revised the gaudier displays of his time and created a manger scene that was true to the Biblical account of Jesus' birth. It helped the people who could not read and write comprehend more of the story of the miracle of His birth.

In Poland children receive gifts twice during the Christmas season. St. Nicholas brings the first gifts on St. Nicholas Day, and the Star Man, with the Star Boys, brings the gifts on Christmas Eve.

In the Czech Republic, the Christmas Eve dinner consists of carp, pudding, and fruit stew. A seat is left vacant at the dinner table for the Christ Child.

Kwanzaa is a celebration that some who are of African-American heritage chose to observe. It is a non-religious holiday celebrated from December 26 through New Year's Day. The custom was begun by Maulana Karnega in 1966, with Kwanzaa meaning the first fruits of the harvest. It is designed to promote a feeling of pride in their heritage. Each of the seven days is assigned a certain principle that is the theme of the day.

Christmas in the Far East is a fairly new celebration. Christianity brought Christmas to the Orient. A small portion of the Chinese celebrate Christmas. Here, trees of light and paper lanterns are intermingled with holly for decorations. Santa is known as Lam Khoong-Khoong meaning "nice old father."

Korea has a small population of Christians who have traditional religious services at Christmas. Children put on pageants and plays depicting the Christmas story. In some churches, people go to church on Christmas Eve and stay there until around 2 A.M. and then go out into the neighborhood singing at the homes. They are often invited in for a treat.

Japan has made Christmas a secular holiday, probably because they make so many decorations for those of us here in the rest of the world. Even those who are not Christians celebrate the secular Christmas. Christmas is an economic and social event for the Japanese who are not Christian.

In countries where Christians make up only a small portion of the population, Christmas celebrations are usually held where missionaries have established a work with the native people. In Africa, Christmas is observed simply. During the holiday season they concentrate on helping those in need. Very little gift giving takes place.

We are truly a blend of many cultures and peoples and the traditions we observe have special meaning to us because of our heritage. The stories that have been passed down through the years from our parents and grandparents have kept them alive.

Arlene Siepmann grew up in South Africa. In her family, the traditions revolved around food. She tells of Christmas in her home in a small town in that country.

"We celebrated with a tree if possible. Evergreens did not grow easily in the tropical climate and so sometimes we could not afford one. Once I remember my dad going out and finding a few bamboo branches that we decorated.

"We never spent time with family for they all lived in another country. We didn't even have close friends with whom we shared time. Dad never felt comfortable having company over to our house so we did not develop the close friends we otherwise would have.

"Much of Christmas revolved around food. The most important item was the Christmas cake and my mom made it several weeks in advance. The fruit cake was very different from the American fruit cakes, only glace cherries as far as glazed fruits were concerned. The only nuts were almonds, blanched and split.

"The cake was baked in a large tin (no hole in the center) with heavy brown paper and then wax wrap to line it since it baked for several hours. Years later when I made my own Christmas cake, I would bake it in a large store-bought cookie tin and cover it with the lid part of the baking time. This made it moist.

"We covered the cake with almond icing (paste) which was 'glued' on with warm apricot jam. The almond paste was rolled out like for rolled cookies, then cut to fit the cake and sealed. The cake never had to be frozen or refrigerated because of the sealing and as it matured, the taste improved. When it was cool and dry, then the Royal Icing was applied—a frosting made with powdered sugar and beaten egg white which caused it to harden when dry.

"We used a special strip of fringed and decorated Christmas paper to go around the side of the cake. On the top we usually placed small ceramic people and other objects along with holly sprigs.

"On Christmas Day we always had a roll of roast beef with potatoes, whole onions, and pumpkin pieces roasted with the meat. Another special that day was bowls of nuts and raisins, which Mom had placed in the living room. This was the only time we could afford nuts.

"One more dish was important—the plum pudding. I remember one time when my grandmother had made it in a cloth immersed in boiling water. Our family always bought one in a little tub. The hostess always pushed tiny 'tickey' coins and small lucky charms into the pudding. One could buy the special charms for the puddings. The plum pudding was served warm with smooth yellow custard.

"Two of the best Christmases I ever had were in the mid 1960s when we were students at Andrews University in Michigan. The only family we had in this part of the world was in California and that was too far to go. My sister, back in Africa, was engaged to a young man who lived with us. He and his brother went up to their aunt's home in northern Michigan and invited us to accompany them. We declined since it was a couple of days before Christmas and the family did not know us.

"A few hours later the aunt called and I remember her words: 'This is Aunt Millie. Get right on up here at once.' We went and never have I felt the warmth and caring as in that home where so many were welcomed. The presents took four hours to open and the food was delicious—but it was the hospitality and love shared with foreigners that I remember the most."

Arlene shared her recipe for this special Christmas cake. Like most fruit cakes, the process to bake one is a little lengthy and involved, yet easy to do. The end product is worth the work.

STAR CHRISTMAS CAKE

(2 pounds)	1 1/2 cups seedless dark or golden raisins
(2 pounds)	2 cups currants
(10 ounces)	2 cups large seeded raisins, halved
(1/4 pound)	2 cup glacé cherries
(2 pounds)	1 cup blanched and split almonds
(2 pounds)	1 1/2 cups diced stoned dates or an extra 2 pounds large raisins
(2 pounds)	1 1/2 cups chopped candied peel
(1.2 pound)	1/2 cup diced preserved ginger
(12 ounce)	3 cups flour
	1 1/2 teaspoons baking powder
	2 teaspoon salt
	1 teaspoon mixed spice
	1 teaspoon ground nutmeg
(2 pounds)	1 cup butter or mixed shortening
(2 pounds)	1 1/4 cups brown sugar
	6 eggs
	1/4 cup marmalade
	1/3 cup strong Roma (a caffeine-free coffee substitute) or sparkling grape juice

In a large bowl, combine fruit, almonds, peel, and ginger.

In a medium bowl, sift together flour, salt, baking powder, and spices; sprinkle over prepared fruit mixture. Mix until each piece is coated.

In a separate large bowl, cream butter (or mixed shortening). Add sugar gradually; beat well. Add eggs one at a time;

beat thoroughly after each addition. Stir in marmalade. Add fruit mixture a little at a time—alternately with the Roma (or sparkling grape juice); mix thoroughly after each addition. Turn into a deep 10-inch round cake pan (or two round 8-inch pans) lined with 3 layers of heavy parchment—the top layer greased with butter. Bake at 300°F for 3 1/2 hours for the large cake—2 3/4 to 3 hours for two smaller cakes. Leave the cake in the pan until cold; wrap in waxed paper. Store in a tin.

HOW TO DECORATE: About two weeks before Christmas, cover cake with almond paste. Leave two or three days to dry thoroughly. Coat whole cake with Royal Icing and let sit twenty-four hours. With a toothpick, outline a six-point star on top of the cake; mark small triangles around edge. With writing tip, pipe short lines between star and triangles. Outline star with three rows of small roses (white, green, white), making three roses from each point of star to edge of cake. Top with red balls. Finish edge of cake with a surround of white and green roses. Outline triangles with white roses. Tie red ribbon around cake and pipe roses around the edge. (This is where the special fringed paper mentioned in the story was used.) Pipe green and white shell edging around base of cake. Decorate with sprays of holly in center triangles.

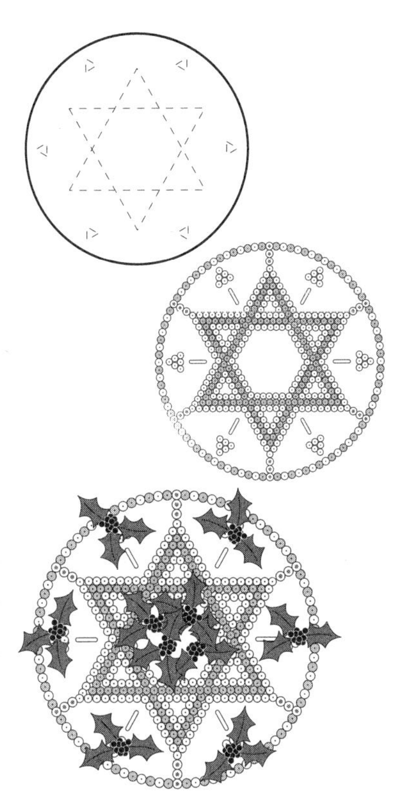

CHRISTMAS IS FOR KIDS . . .

"My favorite thing to do at Christmas is to set up our Nativity Scene. Our Nativity Scene has Mary and Joseph kneeling around Jesus' manger. Then the wise men have their gifts in their hands, the shepherds have their sheep beside them and they're bowing before Him. I'm thankful that Jesus is alive so we can all worship Him."

–Hannah Pearce, Fourth Grade

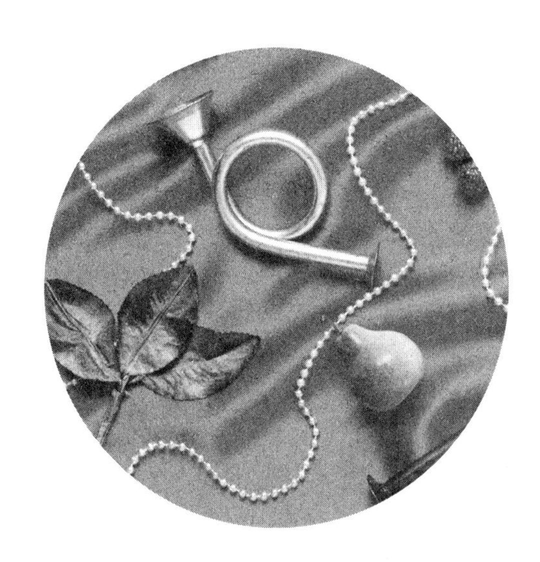

Christmas is a condition of the heart
that continues all year.

Christmas Throughout the Year

Carrying the spirit of Christmas with us throughout the year reminds us why we celebrate the birth of Jesus. The love and generosity that is demonstrated at Christmas overflows into our lives long after the season is past.

Stan and Angie Hardt began a tradition in their home many years ago that carries the Christmas spirit through the year. They keep the Christmas cards they received the past year and each day choose one and reread the letter or message included. During their family worship time, they pray for the individuals who sent the card. (I want to send them a card so that I too will be blessed by having them pray for me and my family.)

Calvin and Barbara Huset also follow this practice and Calvin said they feel they have been blessed by remembering the many family and friends who send them cards each year.

Family relationships are cemented by having elderly aunts, uncles, and cousins spend Christmas with your family. Children have the opportunity to get to know these elderly relatives when they are invited to our homes. Throughout the year, the love relationship that began with the Christmas visit can be encouraged. Shopping trips, picnics, and other activities where these same family members are included give support and encouragement to them and they also will become a support system for our families.

Alma was a cousin of Darrell's mother and in her later years, after she was a widow, she spent many Christmases with us. One year, she and Auntie Agnes came to stay with us for a few days during the Christmas season. We have a tradition that we began when we were newlyweds of spending a few moments in the morning and again in the evening, together as a family, worshiping God. We read a selection of verses from the Bible and include a devotional thought from a favorite book after which we kneel together and pray. After the prayer, upon arising, Darrell and I always embrace and kiss each other.

Alma had never before been invited to share in a family worship time. When Darrell and I embraced, as usual, after our prayer time she was so impressed that she could not forget this expression of love and commitment. She talked about it for years after and shared with her friends what a blessed Christmas it was for her to be a part of a family worship time.

Giving to others fills our hearts during the holiday season and with a little thought this spirit of giving can continue all year. Little things are what are so important in our lives. A little gift of time, a little effort given to helping someone with a task that is too difficult is another way to keep Christmas in our hearts all year.

Christmas is for kids . . .

"I like Christmas because I can see my family. I like giving people gifts and I like celebrating Jesus' birthday, and having a good time.

"The best present I have ever had is the present I am getting this year. It is our new house! We are moving New Year's Day!"

–Meagan Osvold, Fourth Grade

When the joy of Christmas is in our hearts,
it spreads to all around us.

The Joy of the Season

Celebrate Christmas just for the joy of it all! Joy seems to be in short supply on this earth so it is good to take time to live just for the joy of life. "I remember" are two of the favorite words people have used as they shared their joyful Christmas traditions and memories. As long as I live, I will always remember the joy that fills our house during the holiday season. There were seasons when we had more "things" than other years, but things contributed little to the joy we experienced.

Candy Seltman wrote of her memories:

"My strongest memory of my childhood traditions are simply the joy of shared experiences we had as a family. My story can most easily be recalled by my sensory memories. The sense of the tastes, smells and sounds of Christmas are imprinted on my mind. The cold touch of the Minnesota wind on my face as I charged down the hill in the pasture on my sled is one of the many examples within my memory bank.

"My sense of taste involved the enjoyment of food that was part of my mother's Norwegian heritage and also my dad's family traditions. How our mouths would water, as we rode home on the school bus, in anticipation of the goodies mother had made that day. Arriving home, we would find the table covered with plates of lefsa, fattiman, rosettes, fudge, divinity, fruitcake, pop corn balls, sugar cookies or whatever goodies my mother had made that day. She always let us sample the treats before she stored them. How we enjoyed them!

"Even today when I smell cinnamon and cloves it reminds me of walking into my childhood home at Christmas time. The aroma of fresh oranges takes me back to discovering them in my stocking on Christmas morning. The orange was always placed on the very top, the nuts, apples and Christmas candy filled the rest of my brown stocking. The fragrance of pine reminds me of the fresh tree ready to be decorated."

Kay Nelson wrote the following account of her husband Glenn's memories:

"I attended grade school at the Thief River Falls Church School. It was a small school with more boys than girls. During my sixth through eighth grades, Evelyn Wangsnes was my teacher.

"For our Christmas program, Miss Wangsnes found a skit with a story about an older lady. I was chosen to play the part of the elderly lady. Dressed in a dress for this occasion my hair was powdered with baby powder to make it appear gray. They did a good job of putting powder on my hair. When I walked out on the stage, the movement of walking caused the powder to poof into the air. When the air was filled with the powder, it became very noticeable! This brought the house down with laughter.

"The skit was a comical story. I was unaware that the audience was laughing at my powdered hair. I just felt they were laughing at the story. After the program the people shared with me the reason they were laughing. The whole thing became funnier as we laughed together!

"We always enjoyed doing the skits and plays. Our parents brought goodies for refreshments after the program. We students exchanged gifts at this event as well. The local church family joined in to make this a festive time of fun and food. The season of Christmas was a very happy time in our little church school."

I also remember those days when Glenn and his brothers and the other children were so cooperative and joyful as we planned and presented our Christmas programs. The children quickly entered into the joy of the season and together we had a good time.

Lefsa making is another of the joys of the Nelson household. Kay says:

"We as a family make lefsa, a Norwegian delicacy. Lefsa is made from boiled potatoes, which are riced or mashed. Then flour and shortening or cream is added with a little salt and sugar. It is then rolled out flat and thin like a tortilla. It is baked on a special lefsa grill, which is designed to heat up to 500 degrees. You bake the lefsa on a dry, very hot grill.

"We seem to enjoy the tradition of eating it 'hot' off the grill. We prefer real butter on our hot lefsa. Some of us enjoy just plain butter on our rolled up lefsa. Others like sugar, brown sugar, or cinnamon sugar on top of the butter. We usually have a fruit salad with the lefsa.

"My mom, Peggy Laidlaw and sister, Peggy Peterson,

and I all take turns at rolling when there are several family members present. We begin in the early afternoon and keep the lefsa warm by piling it on a heavy plate and covering with towels. It takes a lot of lefsa to satisfy these Norwegians. One can become very weary of rolling and watching the grill. The ummms and ahhhs make it all worthwhile."

Doris Gothard wrote of her "I remember" time as a child.

"I remember Christmas as 'joyful.' As a child growing up in the cotton fields of Alabama, Christmas was the only Holiday of the year! It was and still is, a most memorable time. The focus was on family and fun. Unlike most children today who expect presents under the tree, I knew there was going to be plenty of fruit and good food on the table!

"Christmas was a time to laugh and play, cook and eat. My family was too poor to buy store-bought gifts. But we were rich in handmade gifts. My greatest gift was the gift of time and love that my grandparents gave me. Our family gathered around the large black 'pot-belly' wood burning stove to keep warm, eat Grandma's special cookies and snow ice cream, and hear Grandpa tell stories about our ancestors, this was a 'joyful' time in my life as a child.

"The cookies 'n' snow ice cream were a special family treat, made only at Christmastime in our home. There is no sound quite so deafening as the churning sound of a hand-turned ice cream freezer, filled with ice and rock salt. There is no smell quite as tantalizing as the smell of spice cookies baking in the kitchen, in an old wood stove oven. The thought of those cookies baking in the oven made my sister and me eager to volunteer to help Grandma make the cookies. This family experience of helping Grandma bake cookies in the kitchen at

Christmastime will be remembered for years and years to come.

"During the time of year when Christmas comes, I remember a valuable lesson learned from my childhood upbringing which I have carried into my adult life. Parents don't have to go into debt to give their children great gifts. Just give them homemade cookies 'n' cream, your time and lots of love."

My cousin, Lorraine Payne, says:

"I remember, when I was growing up Mom always made lutefisk and lefsa for Christmas Eve dinner. Along with these two delicacies she made filled Christmas cookies. A sour cream sugar cookie rolled out and filled with a filling made from ground raisins made them very special. The joy of Christmas was celebrated as we ate our tasty meal.

"I love Christmas, the smells of yummy chocolate chip cookies, Mama's pumpkin pies and handmade pralines make my mouth water. The bright sparkling lights on homes, carols being sung by church choirs add to the joy of Christmas. Meeting people whose faces shine with happiness, the annual evening neighborhood drive to see all the homes decorated with lights and Nativity scenes are all part of the joy of Christmas."

"I remember" is an important part of celebrating Christmas just for the joy of the occasion.

Kay Nelson shares her recipe for lefsa.

AGGIE'S LEFSA

- 1 quart (4 cups) cooked, riced, and mashed potatoes
- 2 tablespoons evaporated or regular milk
- 3 tablespoons butter
- 1 cup flour
- 1 teaspoon granulated sugar

Pack potatoes firmly in measuring cup after they are riced. Add milk and butter; mix. Cool to room temperature; add flour and sugar. Roll out on floured pastry cloth—use just enough flour to allow easy rolling. Bake on hot lefsa griddle at 500°F. *A lefsa griddle is a large round griddle made expressly for the purpose of baking lefsa.*

AUTHOR'S NOTE: The "old-timers" used whipping cream instead of butter or shortening and this is what I use. Today some use a combination of cream and shortening. I use the same proportions Kay uses but instead of the milk and butter, I use 2 cups of whipping cream. I also like to use potatoes that have been cooled in the refrigerator—a smaller amount of flour is required and the dough is easier to work.

One time when I was a novice at lefsa making, I mixed all of the ingredients together and left the dough to chill overnight in the refrigerator. In the morning I had the worst mess you can imagine. The dough was almost like a flour paste and so very sticky. I smile now when I think of my learning curve with lefsa baking.

Lefsa should be very tender when done to perfection. My family loves it when mine gets a bit tougher and tell me I spoil it when it is tender like it should be. It has been fun to teach my daughter-in-law and son-in-law the "in's" and "out's" of making this traditional Norwegian treat.

Recipes are like families—they bring joy that should be shared with others! Doris Gothard shared this favorite.

Our Favorite Spice Cookies

6 cups flour
2 cups quick cooking oatmeal
2 cups granulated sugar
1 cup brown sugar
4 teaspoons baking powder
1 teaspoons baking soda
1 teaspoon salt
2 teaspoons cinnamon
1 teaspoon ground cloves
1 teaspoon ground ginger (optional)
1 cup shortening
1 stick butter
3 eggs
1/2 cup molasses
1 cup applesauce
3 cups raisins
3 cups chopped dates
2 cups chopped walnuts

Blend well; chill dough in refrigerator overnight. Drop by tablespoons onto baking sheet; bake at 350°F for 10 to 12 minutes.

Christmas is for kids . . .

"We sit around the Christmas tree and sing songs."

—Ray Daugherty, First Grade

"O Christmas tree, O Christmas tree,
O tree of green, unchanging,
Your boughs, so green in summer time,
Do brave the snow of wintertime"
(GERMAN CAROL).

BRINGING HOME THE TREE

Credit is given to many sources for the origin of the custom of bringing an evergreen into the house and decorating it with candles and brightly colored ornaments. Perhaps the most familiar is the one credited to Martin Luther. It is said that Martin Luther was walking in the woods one night and the starlight caused the snow on the branches of an evergreen to glisten. Thinking this would be a wonderful Christmas decoration, he brought an evergreen home. As a family, he, his wife, and children fashioned candle holders and made other colorful decorations for the tree. Thus was born the tradition of the Christmas tree in German homes.

In North America, the tradition of having a tree began with families who immigrated and brought this holiday tradition with them. Through the years, other cultures and peoples have added their special cultural celebrations to the season.

Many families have a tradition of going into the forest to find a tree that will grace their home. Those who do not live near a forest where they are allowed to harvest trees can go to a tree farm to choose and cut a tree. But the experience is not for everyone.

Francis Wilson shares her experience:

"We have had several live trees purchased from a city lot. One year, while we were visiting friends, we bought a 'ticket' that allowed us to cut a tree for ourselves. So we went hunting for a Christmas tree the day after Thanksgiving in the mountains surrounding Flagstaff, Arizona. We could not find a tree that was shapely enough for all our family to approve, so we gave the unused ticket away.

"We now use an artificial tree each year, which has two advantages: we don't have to search for the 'perfect' tree each year, and the tree is available anytime we have the opportunity to set it up and decorate it."

Rachel Blom Hill remembers her dad and brothers going out into the woods on their farm and cutting a real tree.

"We had some trimmings, but what I remember most are the candle holders we clamped on the tree branches. Medium sized candles were placed in them. Can you imagine the fire danger! Of course, the tree was so fresh there probably wasn't any real danger and I think we just lit them on Christmas Eve while we opened our presents. I know my mom watched it very closely. I would enjoy having some of those candles and the holders today for the memories they bring to mind. Christmas was a family time we all enjoyed."

"From the time I can remember, we never bought a Christmas tree," writes Eddie Heinrich. He added:

"On a Sunday about two weeks before Christmas, we would pack a lunch, put sleeping bags in the back of the truck and head out to the mountains. We kids would wrap-up in sleeping bags and roll around the back of the truck for an hour or two until we got to Platina, California, where there is a forest ranger station. There we got a permit to cut a tree. Sometimes it was a tall scraggly tree and other times it was a short bushy one, but each one was selected after many hours of searching. After the tree was cut, we piled back into the green Chevy truck and rolled around under the tree all the way back home to Igo. We always had a lot of fun at Christmas."

Living for a time in Texas, Barb and Lee Huff and children adopted the local expression of "having their tree." This meant the time you gathered around the tree and opened your gifts. To this day they talk about "having our tree."

My sister-in-law, Kathy tells of living on a farm with many evergreen trees. She recalls going out with her mother to cut just the right tree. "We had a wonderful tree that year and what fun Mom and I had!" She adds:

"Clarence and I were married on December fifteenth and our first Christmas together as husband and wife holds a special place in my heart and in my memory. Right after we came home from our honeymoon we went to town and picked out the tree we wanted and bought groceries and did other shopping. What fun we had putting up our first tree together! Our local druggist had given us a small ornament that had a little spinner inside. When this particular ornament was next to the heat of a bulb, it would spin around and around. It has hung on our tree every year for 36 years. Just this year, I heard our son telling his son how Grandpa and Grandma had been given the little ornament for their first Christmas tree."

Whether short or tall, fresh or artificial, scraggly or full, the tree is an important part of celebrating Christmas. We enjoy the colorful ornaments, the pretty lights, the beauty of colorfully wrapped packages underneath it. The tree becomes the place to sit near and reminisce about family and Christmases past. It has become an established family tradition to have a decorated tree to bring brightness and color to our home.

Christmas is for kids . . .

"I enjoy driving to my grandma's house for Christmas. Our family cuts down a Christmas tree on my grandma's farm."

–Olivia Edelbach, First Grade

Grandmas and Grandpas make Christmas a blessing for everyone.

Going to Grandma and Grandpa's House

"Virgil and I were the first grandchildren of Grandpa and Grandma Rustad and were thrilled to go to their house for Christmas. When I was six years old, they gave us each a white two-blade pocket knife. I was so excited to think that I was 'big enough' to have a knife of my own. I still treasure that knife after nearly seventy years."

This is one of the "I remember" stories my husband shared with his children and now shares with the grandchildren.

RuthAnn MacDonald felt she was reliving some of her childhood as she told of visiting her grandparents at Christmas time.

Going to Baba's for Christmas

The train ride from our hometown to where Baba lived seemed forever to an active, excited seven-year-old girl. We'd see Baba and Grandpa twice a year, at Christmas and again in the summer months. Today we can travel the same distance in forty-five minutes with a car. When I was a child, it took the train more than three hours as it stopped at every little town.

The first task was to pack the suitcase for the two younger sisters, Mother, and myself. Dad drove up to the house with the team of horses pulling a red sleigh with a huge green box half-filled with hay that still had the sweet smell of dried grasses. Wool quilts and a feather tick topped the hay. Dad helped each of us into the box and away we went to the train station. The trip to the station was about five miles that seemed like fifty miles. Once at the station, we said Goodbye to Dad and boarded the train. Before long, the steam locomotive sent out a screaming whistle and we were bound for Baba's house.

The train ride to Baba's town seemed to last for ever. It was dark and we were asleep when we arrived. The train crew helped Mother with her sleeping girls.

Uncle was there to meet us with his sleigh and horses. Snuggled under the feather quilt, Esther, Marie, and I were warm and comfortable. The moonlight provided light for my uncle to guide the horses as we traveled eighteen miles from town to Baba's house. The snow sparkled like diamonds in the moonlight. Mother and Uncle visited all the way home. We children fell asleep somewhere along the way.

I don't remember arriving at Baba's house, but the next morning I was snuggled in a toasty warm bed when I woke up to the sound of laughter and the aroma of baking and cooking. It was the morning of the day of Christmas Eve and time to get out of bed. When I came downstairs, I saw Baba, Uncle Steve, Uncle John, Aunt Annie, Aunt Mary, Mother, and Grandpa all laughing and enjoying each other while preparing the evening meal.

The borscht (beet soup) smelled good enough to make anyone hungry. The goose was dressed and ready for the oven. The Kutia (wheat) was cooked and honey syrup had been poured over it. There was hlubtsi (cabbage rolls) made with rice, onions, garlic, and some buckwheat.

There was naly snyky (cheese rolls) which is cottage cheese rolled up in a crepe topped with thick cream and dill weed. Homemade dill pickles were the ultimate treat. There was also pyroky (perogies) with cottage cheese, potato, or sauerkraut filling, served with creamed onions.

Aunt Annie was making cookies and she let me help her press each dough ball with a fork. I was thrilled to help. If I had my way, I would have filled up on cookies. There were ginger cookies, date squares, and stewed dry fruit. The poppy seed roll, everyone's favorite, was also made and ready for our supper. Then I wished Christmas would come more often than once a year.

Baba always had a wooden box with straw in it under the table. This was to remind us that Christ, the most precious gift God gave us, was born in a stable.

I always felt very special and loved at Baba's house. On a little table in the corner of the living room were three corn husk dolls made by Baba for my sisters and me. Uncle John gave each one of us a bow for our hair. Everyone present received an orange.

This was Christmas at Baba's house in the early 1940s on the prairies in Canada. Now I am a Baba!

When Doris and Eddie Bacon were raising their family, they spent one Christmas with her parents and the next with Ed's parents. "Now," she writes, "our children and families come home every other year as we did. With 22 of us, that is quite a house full! Everyone is so scattered that it's really special when we all get together. Everyone, from the oldest to the youngest, gets involved in performing a play or a song for us."

"When our children were growing, we usually spent part of the holidays traveling to and from one grandparents' house one year and the other grandparents' the next year," said Peggy Tompkins. "We really didn't establish many traditions although we have many memories. Since I wanted our children to be able to celebrate Christmas in their homes, Joel and I spend Christmas Eve with our daughter and her family, then we fly to our son's home for Christmas Day and stay with his family until New Year's Eve."

We also share our grandchildren with their Grandpa and Grandma Schimek. We are fortunate that the kids live next door to us so we are happy they can also spend a part of the holiday season with their other grandparents. One year they spend Christmas Eve and Christmas Day with us and leave the next day to travel to Minneapolis and spend the rest of the holidays with the Schimeks. The next year they go to the Schimeks for Christmas Eve and Christmas Day and return in time to spend a part of the holidays (usually New Year's) with us. Then we have a second "Christmas Eve" when we exchange our gifts and celebrate together. We have chosen to celebrate Christmas Eve at Rod and Dawn's so the children will have memories of Christmas celebrations at their home too. They come to our house for Christmas Day or New Year's.

Our Peggy shared these fond memories:

"My first memories of Christmas Eve are at my grandpa and grandma's house. I know we ate Christmas

Eve supper there, but I don't remember what we ate. I am sure lutefisk and lefsa were there though, because they always are at every Christmas Eve supper. I remember Grandma, Auntie Doris, and Mom washing the dishes after supper and I was sure they washed every dish in the cupboards because it took them forever. You see, that was a very long time because it was only after the dishes were washed that Santa Claus would come."

Grandparents know that Christmas is so much better because they have the grandchildren. Their excitement and enthusiasm is "catching" and puts us all in the Christmas mood. They remind us of the time when our children were little and all of life was ahead of us.

Christmas is for kids . . .

"Christmas means Jesus' birthday. I love Him."

–Felissia Fry, Second Grade

"There is a special joy in giving to those who can't give back."

–Ron Meekma

Extending Christmas Blessings

I don't believe there is another time of the year when people seem so interested in helping others as they are at Christmas. Some people seem to have the gift of making others happy without causing embarrassment or leaving others feeling they need to reciprocate. These people quietly go about doing good and sharing with neighbors, friends, and those who don't bake or cook for themselves.

My mother-in-law had a heart filled with love for those around her. It was important to her to make sure that those who weren't going to be at her home have a little Christmas feast made up of special goodies and other tasty food. Christmas Eve would find her finishing up the last of her "care" packages to be delivered to those she had selected. The bachelors across the road received an ample amount of this good food as did the widower and his son and many others. Guests were sent home with a sampling of cookies and other treats.

My nieces and nephew were very young when they learned of a family who was not going to have much for Christmas. Their home had been destroyed by fire and Kathy and Clarence Wangsnes, and their children, Deanna, Jon, and Brenda all decided together that they would each get only one present and they would give the rest of their Christmas money to this family to use to buy something they needed. Kathy said, "When we took the money and gave it to the mother, her eyes filled with tears. She couldn't believe we were really giving them this money. The family was living in a barn while waiting to find a house again. It left an impression on our children. I wish we had done something like this every year. What a wonderful lesson for us."

Auntie Agnes never let us leave the house without a "little something for the children." Her own sons had died when they were babies and she had a tender heart for children. The "little something for the children" she would send with us was always something that she knew the children would love.

When baking and planning for Christmas and the holiday season, people like my mother-in-law and Auntie Agnes would be sure to make extra so they would have enough to share.

Our Community Service ladies at church prepare special plates with fruit and home baked breads and sweets for those who are house bound and otherwise alone at this season. Mae Howes orchestrates the planning for the baked goods to be given and does much of the baking herself. These are attractively packaged and delivered a few days before Christmas. They are received with appreciation. Other holiday food baskets are given as they find there is a need.

The lefsa that Maude Buchholz has brought to family gatherings is a treat we all have enjoyed. Knowing the labor of love this has been for her makes the lefsa taste extra good.

The tradition of bringing Christmas treats to those who serve our communities on Christmas Eve is a special love gift we can all do. The nurses who leave their families and go to the hospital to care for the patients and staff the emergency room appreciate the extra care that the community extends to them. The same is also true for those working in nursing homes caring for the elderly. Our police officers who work the evening and night shifts have their spirits lifted when they are shown they are appreciated with our gifts of Christmas goodies. We could add the caretakers at group homes and the workers at the local utility company.

Many families work together, preparing and delivering their love gifts. By becoming a part of extending the blessings of Christmas, the holiday is made more enjoyable and more meaningful for all.

"One Christmas there was a boy named Zachary and he loved Christmas. His favorite thing about Christmas was to open presents. And there also was a man named Scrooge and he hated Christmas. Since he hated Christmas so much nobody wanted to be around him and he was also the grumpiest man in the town. Whenever anybody gave him a present, he would just throw it on the ground and stomp into the house. One Christmas someone gave him a present and this time he didn't throw it on the ground and he didn't stomp into the house, but this time he opened it and guess what was inside, it was a puppy! He was so happy! He fed it, he cuddled with it, and he also cared for it. They cared for each other until they both died so they couldn't care for each other anymore. THE END."

–Zachary Graham, Fourth Grade

Santa Claus is coming to town.
Or is he?

What About Santa Claus?

The tradition of Santa Claus bringing gifts to children is an old one that probably has its beginnings in the story of Good Saint Nicholas who gave gifts to the children from poor families. It seems every country has a tradition of someone who is the Christmas giver. These stories have often begun with one individual who was especially generous and went about doing good during the Christmas season. He has been given various names such as, Father Christmas, Kris Kringle, St. Nicholas, and others according to the languages of the various countries. The stories of his graciousness have grown and been added to through the years. It is difficult to tell where truth ends and fiction begins.

Clement C. Moore, a minister, wrote his famous

poem, "A Visit From Saint Nicholas" in 1822. This poem describes the saint more as we know him today. Thomas Nast, the famous American cartoonist, provided the illustrations. The poem and Nast's drawings of Santa with his reindeer and sleigh have become a part of American folklore.

Because we never felt we could tell our children something that was not true, we did not bring them up believing that Santa Claus was real. Surrounded as we are in our culture by the folklore of Santa and his reindeer, we chose to enjoy the story with the children. They always knew who gave them their gifts yet they enjoyed the tradition that had begun in their daddy's family when Uncle Virgil was a baby.

When Virgil and Darrell were little, Dad or one of the uncles who often lived with them would put on a red shirt and a Santa mask and carry a pack that consisted of a pillowcase with a few gifts in it. Santa would then come around the house and knock on the windows and peer in to see them. They would wave and tell him to come to the door so they could see him and get their presents. They always knew who was playing Santa and it was a ritual they enjoyed.

When our children were young, they knew Santa was their cousin David. When Peggy and Rodney got bigger, they took turns being Santa for Judy. They remember the mask as very scratchy. Judy wanted to continue the tradition and be Santa for the rest of us. We have laughed many a time over the funny things that happened with this little tradition. We still have the pillowcase and the mask that made up Santa's costume when Darrell's dad was Santa to his boys.

In my research I have learned that other families tell of the same type of tradition that has been carried on in their families. It is a way for children to enjoy this fun part of Christmas.

Today's children see many Santas in department stores and malls and often have their pictures taken with him. Taking a picture with Santa has become a tradition in many homes.

Reading the history of Christmas in many lands helps us understand where the different customs and practices began. Reading these stories together as a family helps the history of Christmas come alive. Together, families can learn where the tradition of Saint Nicholas—or Santa Claus as we call him in our country—originated. Each family can then make a decision as to what they want to do about Santa Claus.

The beautiful aspect of this tradition is the joy of being the one who gives to others. Gifts given in love bring happiness and joy. Perhaps in a sense, we are all Santa Clauses.

WISE MEN DAY

"As the story of Baby Jesus goes, Wise Men came from a far away place to see Jesus. In our family we have a tradition. After Christmas on the night of January 5 we leave food for the Wise Men and their camels. Then the Wise Men come and take the food and for your kindness leave a gift. Later when you wake in the morning you find a gift from them."

–Brendan Nieta, Seventh Grade

Each family should establish their own traditions that are meaningful to them.

Families and Friends Together

The importance of family traditions is that they bring families together. The time together is spent doing things that are meaningful, delightful, and enjoyable. These may be times of great activity or they may be times of quiet reflection. Many families choose to use family time to read together.

To prepare for Christmas and to help the family think of others, Greg and Robin Berlin always read "The Last Straw" by Paula McDonald Palangi, which is a Christmas story they first read in *Good Housekeeping* magazine. It is also found in Joe L. Wheeler's book, *Christmas in My Heart,* Volume 2. They told me they first read it before they had children and have continued reading it for twelve years. Their children look forward to hearing this story each year.

On Christmas morning the Berlin family gathers for family worship and reads the story of Jesus' birth as found in Luke 2:1-20.

My friend, Doris Bacon, says:

"About a month before Christmas we begin reading an uplifting Christmas story each morning. This helps us remember what Christmas is all about and what we really need to do for others. Besides, with no little kids around to keep reminding us it is almost Christmas, reading these stories puts us in the mood for Christmas even when temperatures are in the 40s and there is no snow at the end of November in Northern Minnesota."

I do believe that the arrival of snow helps those of us who live in the north, get in the spirit of Christmas. We love having a white Christmas with the snow providing a "Currier and Ives" picture-perfect scene.

Christmas carols played on the stereo make the house seem more "Christmassy." The Greg and Robin Berlin family report that they sing Christmas carols whenever they are in the car together. Several families find a time of singing puts Christmas in perspective and they are more relaxed and look forward to the big day with less stress.

Watching the movie "White Christmas" is another tradition of the Berlin family as well as many other families. Driving through the neighborhood enjoying the lighting displays of the various homes is still a tradition many families enjoy. Many come home to enjoy hot chocolate and an evening of conversation while sitting around their tree. Singing familiar carols is a fitting close to these evenings of the holiday season.

You may wish to develop a special tradition that will be based upon an event that happened in your family or because you think it would be meaningful and fun for you to do together.

I like the story mentioned above ("The Last Straw" by Paula Palangi) about the quarreling family whose mother despaired of getting them to stop. Their home definitely did not have the Christmas spirit. She remembered an old custom and decided to give it a try. Gathering the children together she asked if they would like to start a new tradition. She explained to them that it was a game, but it could only be played while keeping it secret.

They were to make a bed in the cradle where they would put a doll representing Baby Jesus. To fill the cradle with straw, each person was to do something nice for another person without them knowing who did the kind deed. When they did this deed, they could place one straw in the cradle. It became a game with them and the whole family entered into the excitement of it. I won't give away the rest of the story because it is just so touching. Even if you haven't read the story you can do the same in your home and begin a tradition of kind acts done for each other in secret.

A small tree decorated with wrapped candies placed by the front door welcomes guests to your home. When the guests leave they are welcome to take a candy with them as a token of hospitality. The same could be done with a wreath made of wrapped candies hung by the door. A pair of scissors may be needed nearby to cut the candies from the wreath. As the season ends, remember the many friends who came and enjoyed the warmth of your home and say a prayer for their happiness and well-being.

Eating and sharing food and meals has become a significant part of hospitality and we all enjoy having guests share with us. A Danish tradition is that no one should leave a home during the Christmas season without having something to eat. Small cookies are placed on a tray or plate for guests to partake of as they leave the house.

A small tree on a hall table decorated with edible cookies, baked and decorated as Christmas tree ornaments is an attractive way to display your handiwork and also to share a bit of goodness with your guests as they leave your home.

Our friend Orlene Amundson paid our family the finest tribute when she wrote in her letter of Christmas remembrances, "I really don't know what to tell you about Christmas memories, most of them center around you and your family in Minnesota."

The memories of our families spending many Christmas holidays at each other's homes are marvelous. Orlene is one of the finest hostesses I have known. Her home was and still is open to everyone. Friends like this cannot be replaced. Family and friends are the best part of Christmas.

Christmas is for kids . . .

"I think Christmas is all about sharing. Every year my mom or dad reads the story about Mary and Joseph traveling to Bethlehem to be counted and when Baby Jesus was born on Christmas day we eat supper then open our presents. Sometimes we watch a Christmas movie."

–Kayla Haugen, Fifth Grade

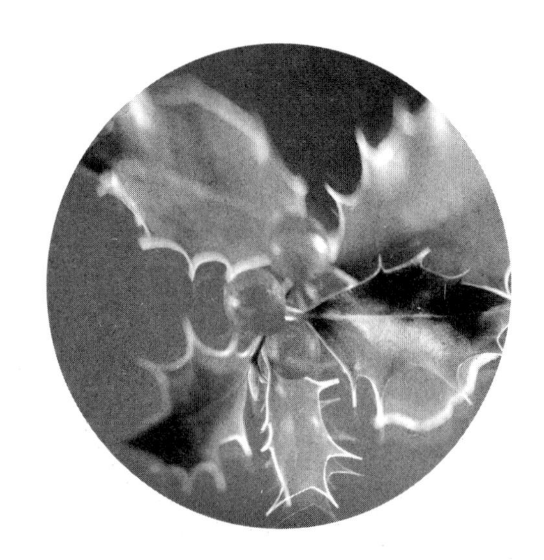

"Deck the halls with boughs of holly,
Fa la la la la, la la la la."
CHRISTMAS CAROL

THE COLORS AND GLITZ OF CHRISTMAS

There is something warm and inviting about a house that is attractively decorated with the bright cheery colors of Christmas. Some families develop traditions based on creating Christmas ornaments and arrangements. Simple things can be made beautiful and reused year after year. Each person's talents can be utilized and enjoyed. Decorations that would be considered "too much" at other times of the year are delightful at Christmas.

Christmas decorations go up inside the house and outside. Some of the earliest to go up for many people are the outdoor lights. These often are put up before the temperatures fall very low, because fingers don't get so cold holding the lights and hanging them on their hooks. Lighted homes evoke warm feelings and a spirit of "Christmas is here!"

Indoors, I like to have a little bit of Christmas in each room. It may be a small tree, a wall hanging, or a table arrangement that will remind us of the joy of the season.

Through the years, we have created many of our own ornaments as family projects. Many were special one-on-one projects between Mom and one of the children. When the children were members of their Pathfinder Club, they made macramé wreaths, about three inches in diameter, of green macramé cord. Another year, Judy made small wreaths in various colors of glass beads strung on florist wire and finished with a ribbon bow. She also cross stitched small stockings from a kit. These and more are on our tree each year.

My friend, Lucille, makes attractive centerpieces from natural greens, enhanced with colorful Christmas leaves and sprays from the craft store. When the arrangements are complete, she adds colorful bows using various ribbons. They make wonderful gifts and door prizes for the organizations to which she donates them.

A centerpiece that I have enjoyed for years was created for me in an old aluminum teakettle. I took it to the local florist and she created an arrangement that is useable season after season. Another is in a beautiful vase and was given to me by my mother-in-law nearly forty years ago. The vase has a three-dimensional scene in a recess on the front and is filled with a blue and green arrangement. I have had to renew the ribbon and a few of the "greens," but basically it is still the same as the original gift.

As I visit in homes, I see so many clever ideas of attractive decorations made without a great expenditure. You may wish to duplicate some of the ideas in this chapter. If your talent is not tying bows or whatever, enlist the help of a friend.

Sprays of fresh or artificial evergreen boughs highlighted with a bright ribbon are hung over the doorways. Antique dishes are used to serve special holiday dishes. Large glass bowls are filled with colored Christmas balls and a little gold or silver glitter or confetti sprinkled among them and used for a centerpiece.

Inexpensive mirror tiles are used effectively as a base upon which to place a centerpiece or arrangement on the table. Candles, large and small, arranged with ribbons and/or ivy intertwining at their base look attractive on these mirrors. Birch logs with holes drilled to hold candles, green boughs and red bows, or small Christmas balls makes a Yule log centerpiece.

Greenery woven around the arms of chandeliers coupled with sparkly balls or ribbons is easy to do. Garlands draped down the staircase railing and over doorways, with small white lights and large bows look great. Mirrors with ribbons wrapped around package style add a festive look.

Sugared fruit in a clear glass bowl is an old Christmas tradition. To sugar fruit, spread egg white on the fruit and then roll the fruit in sugar and allow it to dry. Then place the fruit in a bowl and admire your handiwork.

Glass balls designed for use on a tree are inexpensive and can be used in many ways. They can be covered with glue, rolled in glitter, allowed to dry and then used on the tree or arranged in bowls to sit on end tables. Use fabric paint to write names or other messages on the ball. These can be used for place cards, party favors, or take-home gifts.

Gift baskets filled with holiday breads, herbal teas, homemade candy, small gifts, etc. wrapped in colored cellophane with a pretty ribbon can be made up in advance of the holiday and used as gifts for drop-in guests. Jars of homemade jellies and jams capped with a colorful fabric and tied with a rickrack bow can also be prepared to use for last minute gifts.

Place cards have been a tradition at our home for Christmas dinner. When the children became old enough to help, they worked with me to prepare them. Later they took over this task and made ones that were decorated creatively. Now the grandchildren help with this tradition.

Calligraphy, yarn, marking pens, and colored ink can be used to write the names on the cards. The cards can be made of parchment paper with the edges torn and singed by a candle. White card stock or heavy paper with designs hand-drawn works well. For those who think they have no artistic ability, colorful stickers to fit the season can be used. Hand-quilled designs made of quilling paper and crocheted wreaths mounted on heavy cards are keepsakes for the guests.

Children enjoy making unique gift-wrap. They can use white or brown paper to draw and paint their own designs. Magic markers, water colors, acrylics, fabric paints all can be used to decorate the paper. An old tradition of making potato prints can be a part of the holiday fun. Cut potatoes with a three-dimensional design cut into each side are dipped in paint and then stamped onto the paper.

Decorating our homes expresses our individual personalities. There are those who like one color theme throughout the house, others have a different color theme in each room. Little things are what make Christmas complete. Little details add an ambiance of caring, love, and cheer.

I have a philosophy that I will use my very best china and crystal often and especially during the holiday. With tongue in cheek, I say, "I am not going to save my pretty things for Mrs. Number Two! I want to enjoy them myself with my family." There is no one who is better or more important than your family, so use and enjoy your pretty things at every opportunity.

Family and friends are worthy of our finest and our most thoughtful attention and time. They are why we enjoy the celebration of Christmas.

Christmas is for kids . . .

"What Christmas means to me. Christmas is the best time of year. Because you learn about Jesus' birth. It's Jesus' birthday. Jesus is born. It's a Holy day. We get presents. We decorate the Christmas tree."

–Caleb Osvold, Second Grade

Wedding bells are ringing.

CHRISTMAS WEDDINGS

What a beautiful time of the year to have a wedding! The possibilities for decorations and colors are endless. The Christmas weddings I have attended have been so very original in their decor and the foods that have been served. Meaningful traditions are often begun when weddings take place during the holiday season. Let me share my memories of a few of them.

Clarence and Kathy Wangsnes's mid-December wedding in 1963 was the first wedding I attended that had a Christmas theme using red and white with gold accents. Her mother, Maude Buchholz, made all of the dresses including the bride's gown. The bridal bouquet was white and red carnations with gold balls and holly. Bridesmaid dresses with red velvet bodices and white skirts trimmed with red bows created a festive holiday setting. Floral pieces followed the theme of red and white. A cake decorated all in white with sugar bells and the traditional bride and groom top was the centerpiece for the reception. Delicious Christmas goodies handmade by her mother were served to the guests at the reception.

Juanette and Jerry Juhl's daughter, Tami, married Mike Boyd in a Christmas wedding in the Grand Forks, North Dakota church. Entering the church, we were greeted with a scene of trees in the entry decorated simply with white lights. The sanctuary had two trees again decorated only with white lights. Christmas wreaths hung on the walls to either side of the rostrum. Garlands of greenery, decorated in the bride's colors of gold and burgundy, were hung along the front near the organ and the piano. A beautiful bouquet of flowers with wood twigs sprayed white was on the ledge in front of the baptistry. Candelabra with white and gold tulle and bouquets were fastened on the ends of the pews along the center aisle.

The bride carried a traditional bouquet of white roses and looked radiant in this picture-perfect setting as Jerry, her father, gave her in marriage to Mike. The bridesmaids wore white muffs topped with burgundy roses, evergreen sprays and little white flowers nestled in tulle, which complimented their burgundy dresses so well.

Draped from the ceiling of the reception hall were garlands of greenery decorated with gold and burgundy colored balls, in groups of three, with gold lamé bows and white lights. Christmas trees were grouped in clusters in different areas of the hall. The florist had sprayed the trees with a white sparkly spray and surrounded their bases by white batting to resemble snow. Again these trees were decorated only with white lights. Situated in the different areas near the groupings of trees were park benches. I felt I had walked into the land of

Christmas dreams.

The bride does not especially like cake and wanted cheesecake instead of the traditional wedding cake. Juanette began weeks before the wedding to bake the cheesecakes and freeze them in preparation for the reception. A table covered with a burgundy cloth held stands of various heights upon which the thirty cheesecakes of different flavors were displayed. Each stand was covered with a separate little tablecloth of burgundy with an overlay of gold lamé.

The cheesecakes, each beautifully decorated according to its flavor, were identified by a sign written in calligraphy on a card and placed by each cake. Each cake was then surrounded by a ring of holly. In a large crystal bowl in the center of the table, miniature popcorn balls individually wrapped in clear cellophane tied with gold ribbon added more color and beauty. As the guests came through line, they were served a piece of cheesecake in the flavor they chose. It was so attractive I just enjoyed standing and looking at the tableau that was arranged so well.

Darrell and I were married on December 30 and decided to not do a Christmas theme. However, at the reception we served traditional Christmas goodies. My mother-in-law and her cousin Esther both loved to bake and decided to give us the gift of their Scandinavian baking expertise. Along with the traditional cake, we had a beautiful array of cookies, fattiman, rosettes, lefsa, and other delicacies arranged on round silver trays. A feast for the eye and the stomach.

Candy and Tim O'Toole also had a Christmas wedding in the Grand Forks, North Dakota church. Theirs was a Victorian Christmas theme. Large pink ribbon bows streaming from the top down and white lights accented the twin trees at the front of the church. Dried, pink roses nestled in lace with pink ribbon bows were used as decorations along with pine cones which had been sprayed silver. The bows on the pews were made of pink ribbon with dried roses in the centers accented by artificial evergreens, eucalyptus branches, and sprigs of pearl. Lester Juhl was a proud and happy father as he escorted his lovely daughter down the aisle in a tastefully decorated church.

Candy's sister-in-law, Merriam Juhl had dried the roses in the summer and made the decorations. She also made the bridesmaids' bouquets that consisted of small wooden twigs that were sprayed white with a silver glitter added. To the twigs were added dried pink roses of varying shades with small silver pine cones and pink ribbons. The bouquets were designed to be carried on their arms.

Since the reception was held at a local hotel, which had a well-decorated reception room, they did not add to those decorations. The colorful display of food was the only decoration that was needed to complete the trimmings for the reception. A strawberry marble and chocolate marble cake with strawberry filling was iced in pale pink icing sprinkled with edible iridescent glitter.

On the cake, Merriam used pink ribbon roses set off with artificial greens. To crown the cake, a porcelain bride and groom music box was placed on the top. Sand bakkels, lefsa, spritz cookies, and other colorful Christmas goodies were served on crystal platters garnished by sugar cubes decorated with a piped icing pink flower, a dot of yellow added for the center and a green leaf. Candy and her mother Hilda Juhl had made the Christmas goodies ahead of time and frozen them so they were fresh and oh, so very tasty.

The pew bows are still being used to decorate Candy and Tim's home. She replaced the dried roses with artificial ones and uses them as decorating accents in her guest bedroom. Tim's mother has also used them to add color and beauty to a stairway garland during the

Christmas season.

Tim was in the military when they got married, so it was off to Hawaii where he was to be stationed. While at work, Tim met a young couple and the four of them became friends. They also got to know their friends' parents. For the O'Tooles' first tree, the parents of their friends made them a little gold spider ornament. Each year as they prepare to decorate their tree, the first ornament they get out is the little gold spider. Then they go to the telephone and call the people who made the spider. Candy and Tim again tell these lovely people how much they love them and how much the memory of their gift means to them. What a lovely tradition of warmth and love.

To me, it is beautiful to think of a Christmas wedding being the occasion when a new home is established, a home that will develop its own traditions for Christmas and other days.

Christmas is for kids . . .

"I enjoy opening Christmas presents on Christmas Eve."

–Amanda Jacob, First Grade

"A feast is made for laughter"
(ECCLESIASTES 10:19).

MMM—MMM! GOOD!

As I read the responses to my requests for people to share their family Christmas traditions, I found many of the traditions revolve around favorite foods served each year. Even foods you don't particularly like are served because they bring back memories of someone who really enjoyed that particular dish and it was a firm tradition in your family. The dish may serve as a reminder of a special time when love and happiness was present. Other foods are just so very good that you long to taste them again.

Many of those of Norwegian descent began Christmas with a Christmas Eve supper that had as the featured main dishes both lutefisk and lefsa. To those of us who grew up with this tradition, a small serving of lutefisk served with melted butter and lefsa makes our hearts go home for Christmas. Never mind that the younger members of the family do not enjoy the lutefisk. Lefsa is usually loved by all who have the opportunity to taste this delicacy.

Nola Horne who lives in Monroe, Louisiana writes: "In our family, we try to clean our palates for the big Christmas meal by having Mexican food on Christmas Eve as we gather to open our gifts. In the south, turkey and dressing is the norm from Thanksgiving through Christmas. In fact, we seldom have dressing any other time of the year."

When families gather, the "feast" is often the center of our celebrations. Days are spent preparing everything so the "feast" will live up to our expectations. We partake of our "feasts" enjoying the foods God has provided for our pleasure.

Many people have shared the favorite recipes of their families for this book. They range from main dishes to the goodies we all like. Francis Wilson mentioned the varied dishes she prepares for her family according to each person's favorite. I smiled when reading her list:

- Worthington's dinner roast (for my grandsons)
- Candied sweet potatoes (for my husband)
- Waldorf salad (for my daughter)
- Mashed potatoes (for my husband)
- Squash (for my daughter-in-law)
- Cranberry sauce (for my husband)
- A green vegetable (for me)
- Pumpkin pie (for my son)
- Apple pie (for my son-in-law)
- Cranberry pie (for me)

Her list reminds me of every family I know. We all make the special things each member enjoys. Food is the yummy, good part of Christmas.

Recipes are fun to share and each person makes the recipe their own with slight variations and added ingredients. I have included just a few of the favorites from the contributors to this book. I hope you will try these recipes, savor the smells as they are cooking and baking, and enjoy the taste as you gather around your family dinner tables. Enjoy your special foods because they bring back memories and are a part of what makes Christmas special to you and your families.

◆ ◆

Rilda Pengra whose mother, Pearl, always had "room in the inn" sent her recipe for a traditional cranberry relish.

Cranberry-onion Relish

4 cups whole fresh or frozen cranberries
1 box brown sugar
1 1/2 cups rings of raw white onion
2 cups water
1 tablespoon salt
2 tablespoons Worcestershire sauce
1/8 teaspoon pepper (optional)

In a large saucepan over low heat, combine all ingredients. Stir constantly as juice oozes out. Simmer 10 minutes or until onions are tender. Can be served warm or chilled.

Barbara Huff mentions pecan patties, wild rice, and this Sweet Potato Delight as favorites of her family each Christmas.

Sweet Potato Delight

3 cups mashed sweet potatoes
1/2 cup cream
2 tablespoons butter
Salt to taste
Brown sugar to taste
2 eggs, separated
1/2 cup chopped nuts
(pecans or walnuts are best)

In a large bowl, combine sweet potatoes, cream, butter, salt, and sugar.

In a small bowl, beat egg yolks until frothy; add to sweet potato mixture.

In a separate small bowl, beat egg whites until stiff; fold into sweet potato mixture. Gently stir in nuts. Spoon sweet potatoes into a greased baking dish. Bake at 350°F for 20 minutes or until thoroughly heated.

♦ ♦

Greg and Robin Berlin have a tradition of serving a vegetarian chicken-style loaf.

Chicken-style Loaf

1 can cream of celery soup
1/2 cup canned milk
1 13-ounce can *Worthington® FriChik®*, drained and diced (reserve liquid)
2 eggs
1 package seasoned bread crumbs
1 tablespoon dried, minced onion
2 tablespoons cooking oil

In a large bowl, combine celery soup, milk, and *FriChik®* liquid. Mix in eggs; add bread crumbs, *FriChik®* pieces, onion, and oil. Bake in an greased loaf pan at 350°F for about 45 minutes.

Many people choose to follow a vegetarian diet. (Some of the more unusual ingredients in these recipes may be found at your local natural foods store.) Ardis Stenbakken sent this recipe for a vegetarian main dish. Children will love the novelty of these "turkey legs."

"Turkey Legs"

- 4 eggs
- 3/4 cup bean sprouts, well drained
- 1 cup chopped nuts
- 1 cup chopped mushrooms
- 1 cup grated mild cheddar cheese or dry cottage cheese
- 2 teaspoon celery salt
- 1 tablespoon G. Washington seasoning or chicken-style seasoning
- 1 teaspoon chopped parsley
- 1 diced onion
- 1 cup vegetarian burger
- 1 teaspoon Smokene or liquid smoke
- 2 cups dry bread crumbs

Combine all ingredients. Form into drumstick shapes around 6-inch wooden dowels; deep-fry at 370° to 380°F or bake at 350°F for 20 to 30 minutes. *They taste best if deep-fried.* Serve with chicken-style gravy.

We have eaten so many good meals at Orlene's house. Her cooking expertise always impresses her guests. She shares a recipe that we have enjoyed many times when visiting at her house.

MOCK TURKEY ROAST WITH GRAVY

1 large onion, diced
1 stalk celery, diced
1 heaping tablespoon McKay's chicken-style seasoning
3 eggs, beaten
2 cups uncooked oatmeal
2 tablespoons oil
1 cup cottage cheese
1 cup chopped walnuts (or pecans)
2 cups *Worthington® Diced Chik®**, drained
1/2 cup asparagus juice
1/2 cup sour cream
2 cups milk (approximate)
1/2 cup asparagus juice
2 tablespoons cornstarch
2 teaspoons McKay's chicken-style seasoning
1 package golden G. Washington broth

In a medium skillet over medium heat, saute onion and celery until tender.

In a large bowl, add onion and celery to 1 tablespoon chicken-style seasoning, eggs, oatmeal, oil, cottage cheese, chopped nuts, *Diced Chik®*, 1/2 cup asparagus juice, and sour cream. Mix well; place in a loaf pan. Bake at 350°F for 1 hour.

**Worthington® Diced Chik®* is a soy product available in cans at your local Adventist Book Center or health food store.

GRAVY: In a medium saucepan, combine 1/2 cup asparagus juice and milk. Mix cornstarch with a little water; stir until all lumps dissolve, then add to asparagus juice mixture. Add seasonings; heat to boiling over medium heat. Stir until thickened

When Mock Turkey is done baking, slice and spread over a bread dressing which has been baked in a casserole dish and turned out onto a platter. Drizzle with some asparagus juice gravy.

✦ ✦

Cottage Cheese Loaf is a favorite of my husband. He prefers this simple dish to others that are more involved and time-consuming to make.

COTTAGE CHEESE LOAF

1 large onion
1 stick (1/2 cup) margarine
1 22-ounce carton cottage cheese
5 to 6 cups of Special K cereal
3 packages brown G. Washington Broth
1/2 cup walnuts or pecans, ground or chopped
5 beaten eggs

In a large bowl, combine all ingredients. Mix until evenly distributed; scoop into a greased 9" x 13" glass baking dish. Bake at 325°F for 45 minutes to one hour, depending on your oven. (My family prefers it a little crispy on the outside.) To serve, cut into squares; place on a platter. Garnish with parsley or celery leaves.

Another recipe Ardis Stenbakken and her family enjoy is this coffeecake:

Rich Cherry Walnut Coffeecake

5 to 5 1/2 cups unsifted flour
1/4 cup sugar
1 teaspoon salt
1 teaspoon lemon zest
2 packages active dry yeast
1 cup milk
2 cup water
1 cup (2 sticks) margarine
2 eggs (at room temperature)
2 cups chopped walnuts
2/3 cup maraschino cherries
3 tablespoons sugar
Confectioner's sugar frosting
(this is especially good with a little almond flavoring)

In a large bowl, thoroughly combine 2 cups flour, 1/4 cup sugar, salt, lemon zest, and undissolved dry yeast.

In a saucepan over low heat, combine milk, water, and margarine; stir until very warm (120° to 130°F). *Margarine may not melt completely.* Gradually add to dry ingredients; beat 2 minutes with an electric mixer at medium speed, scraping bowl occasionally. Add eggs and 2 cups flour; beat at high speed 2 minutes, again scraping occasionally. Stir in enough additional flour to make a stiff dough. Cover bowl with plastic wrap, then a towel. Set aside for 20 minutes.

In a medium bowl, combine walnuts, cherries, and 3 tablespoons sugar.

Turn dough out onto heavily floured board; divide in half. Roll each half into a 14" x 10" rectangle; spread with cherry filling. Roll up from long side—as for a jelly roll—to form a 14-inch-long roll. Pinch seam to seal. Place on a greased baking sheet. Cut diagonal slits about 1 inch apart in rolls, starting from top surface of roll and cutting about

2/3 of the way through. Pull cut pieces out alternately right and left (or the roll can be shaped into a wreath after cutting). Cover loosely with waxed paper brushed with oil, then cover with plastic wrap. Refrigerate 2 to 24 hours.

When ready to bake, remove from refrigerator; uncover dough carefully. Let stand at room temperature for 10 minutes. Bake at 375°F for 25 to 30 minutes or until golden brown. Remove from baking sheets; cool on wire racks. Frost with confectioner's sugar frosting. Enjoy!

✦ ✦

Francis' Cranberry Pie

2 cups fresh cranberries
2 cups chopped walnuts or pecans
2 cups granulated sugar
2 eggs
1 cup granulated sugar
1 cup flour
3/4 cup margarine, melted

Spray a 10-inch pie plate with a cooking spray. Spread cranberries over the bottom of the plate. Sprinkle with nuts and 2 cups sugar.

In a small bowl, beat eggs well. Gradually add 1 cup sugar; beat until thoroughly mixed. Add flour and melted butter to egg-sugar mixture; beat well. Pour batter over top of cranberries. Bake at 325°F for 60 minutes or until the crust is golden brown. Cut like pie. Serve either warm or cold; top with vanilla ice cream, if desired. *Francis said they often have this pastry for breakfast.*

Pumpkin cheesecake, the very name sounds delicious. Glenda Nelson, sister of Janean and daughter of Kay, uses the following recipe when she makes this yummy sounding dessert.

Pumpkin Cheesecake

1/4 cup graham cracker crumbs
1/2 cup finely chopped pecans
1/4 cup firmly packed light brown sugar
1/4 cup granulated sugar
1/2 stick (1/4 cup) unsalted butter, melted and cooled to room temp.
1 1/2 cups solid pack pumpkin
3 large eggs
1 1/2 teaspoons cinnamon
2 teaspoon nutmeg
2 teaspoon ground ginger
1/2 teaspoon salt
1/2 cup firmly packed light brown sugar
3 8-ounce packages cream cheese, softened
1/2 cup granulated sugar
2 tablespoons heavy cream
1 tablespoon cornstarch
1 teaspoon vanilla
2 cups sour cream
2 tablespoons granulated sugar
16 whole pecans (for garnish)

Preheat oven to 350°F.

Crust: In a medium bowl, combine graham cracker crumbs, chopped pecans, 1/4 cup brown sugar, and 1/4 cup granulated sugar. Stir in butter; press the mixture into the bottom and 2 inches up the side of a buttered 9-inch spring-form pan. Chill for 1 hour.

Filling: In a large bowl, whisk together pumpkin, eggs, spices, and 1/2 cup brown sugar.

In a separate large bowl, cream together cream cheese and 1/2 cup granulated sugar with an electric mixer. Beat in cream, cornstarch, vanilla, and pumpkin mixture until smooth. Pour filling into crust; bake in middle of oven for 50 to 55 minutes or until the center is just set. Let cool in the pan on a rack for 5 minutes.

TOPPING: In a small bowl, whisk together sour cream and 2 tablespoons granulated sugar. Spread over the top of the cheesecake; return to oven for 5 more minutes. Let cool in the pan on a rack. Cover; chill overnight. Remove the side of the pan; garnish cheesecake with pecan halves.

◆ ◆

Soon after Nancy Kyte was married, she learned about a long-standing Christmas tradition in the Kyte family. Her mother-in-law, Dorothy Kyte, got the recipe for Shortbread Cookies from her best friend, whose mother came from Scotland. They always had Shortbread Cookies, but only at Christmas.

SHORTBREAD COOKIES

1 pound sweet cream butter (do not use margarine)
1 1/2 cups powdered sugar
1 egg yolk (discard white)
4 1/2 cups flour
Colored granulated sugar (to decorate)

In a large bowl, cream together butter and powdered sugar. Add egg yolk and 2 1/2 cups flour. Gradually mix in remaining 2 cups flour. *The dough will be stiff.* Roll out on a clean countertop. (TIP: Placing a sheet of waxed paper over the dough makes it a lot easier to roll out.) Cut into shapes; sprinkle with colored sugar. *Makes 4 dozen.*

Bake at 300-325°F for 15 to 20 minutes. *Do not let them get brown.* These cookies freeze well.

Stollen is a recipe of German origin the Wilsons enjoy. It is made from a basic sweet roll dough and nuts and fruit.

STOLLEN

- 1 cup milk, lukewarm
- 1/4 cup granulated sugar
- 1 teaspoon salt
- 1 package yeast (1 tablespoon)
- 1 egg
- 1/4 cup soft shortening
- 3 to 3 1/2 cups sifted flour
- 2 cups blanched almonds
- 1/4 cup diced citron
- 1/4 cup diced candied cherries
- 1 cup seedless raisins
- 1 tablespoon lemon zest

In a large bowl, mix milk, sugar, and salt. Add yeast; stir until dissolved. Stir in egg and shortening. Add flour gradually, mixing with a spoon first, then with your hands. While kneading, add enough flour to make dough smooth and elastic. Place in an oiled bowl. Cover; let rise until doubled. Punch down; allow to rise again.

Turn dough onto lightly floured board; flatten. Add almonds, citron, cherries, raisins, and lemon rind; knead nuts and fruit into the dough. Pat dough into an 8" x 12" oval; spread with soft margarine. Fold in half the long way; form into a crescent shape. Press folded edges together firmly so the dough won't spring open while baking. Place on lightly greased, heavy baking sheet. Brush top with melted margarine. Let rise until doubled—35 to 45 minutes. Bake at 375°F for 30 to 35 minutes. Frost with confectioner's sugar icing while Stollen is still warm. Decorate with cherries, almonds, and pieces of citron.

Apple bars are a favorite of Janean Nelson.

APPLE BARS

2 1/2 cups flour
1 tablespoon granulated sugar
1 teaspoon salt
1 cup shortening
Milk (+ egg yolk = 2/3 cup)
1 egg yolk
3/4 cups crushed corn flakes

3 to 4 baking apples, pared and sliced
1 cup granulated sugar
1 tablespoon margarine
1 teaspoon cinnamon
1/4 teaspoon nutmeg
1 cup powdered sugar
2 tablespoons hot tap water

In a large bowl, sift together flour, 1 tablespoon sugar, and salt. Cut in shortening. Add enough milk to egg yolk to make 2/3 cup. Divide dough in half. Place one half on jelly roll pan (the smaller the pan, the thicker the crust will be); press out to edges. Sprinkle corn flake crumbs on crust. Place sliced apples on top.

TOPPING: In a small bowl, mix 1 cup sugar, margarine, and spices; sprinkle over apples. Place remaining half of dough on top; seal edges to prevent leaking in oven. Bake at 325°F for 1 hour.

GLAZE: In a small bowl, mix powdered sugar with hot water. Glaze while still hot. Cut into bars.

Cousin Lorraine sent this recipe for:

GRANDMA WALLER'S WHITE SUGAR COOKIES

2 cups granulated sugar
1/2 cup shortening
1/2 cup butter
2 eggs, beaten
1 cup sour cream
1 teaspoon baking soda (mix into sour cream)

6 cups flour, sifted
1 tablespoon flour
1 cup granulated sugar
1 cup boiling water
2 cups ground seedless raisins or dates

In a large bowl, cream together 2 cups sugar, shortening, and butter. Add eggs, sour cream-baking soda mixture, and 6 cups flour; mix until dough is easy to handle. Roll out on a floured surface; cut into circles with a cookie or biscuit cutter.

FILLING: In a medium saucepan, combine 1 tablespoon flour and 1 cup sugar. Stir in 1 cup boiling water. Bring mixture to a slow boil. Add raisins or dates; boil slowly until thick enough to spread on cookies. Cover filling with another cookie; seal edges with a fork. Or, put filling on half a cookie and fold other edge over—making a half-round—again sealing the edges with a fork. Bake at 425°F for 5 to 10 minutes. *Very good!*

Preparing for her traditional Christmas Open House, Becky Carlisle serves many delicious cookies and candies. The following recipes are three that are representative of those she serves and you can be sure they are favorites of everyone who tastes them.

CREAM WAFERS

1 cup butter
1/3 cup whipping cream
2 cups flour
3/4 cup powdered sugar
1/4 cup soft butter
1 teaspoon vanilla
Paste food coloring (optional)

WAFERS: In a large bowl, blend 1 cup butter, cream, and flour. Roll out and cut into 1 1/2" circles (or any size or shape you choose). Dip in granulated sugar on both sides. Bake at 375°F for 7 to 9 minutes.

FILLING: In a medium bowl, combine sugar, 1/4 cup butter, and vanilla; mix well. Add food coloring if desired. Spread filling between two wafers to make a sandwich cookie.

Makes 5 dozen 1 1/2" cookies.

Christmas Cake Cookies

2 1/2 cups sifted flour
1 teaspoon baking soda
1 teaspoon salt
1 teaspoon cinnamon
1 cup butter
1 1/2 cup granulated sugar
2 eggs
2 pounds dates (about 1 lb. if pitted), diced
1/2 pound candied cherries, diced
1/2 pound candied pineapple, diced
1/2 pound almonds, shelled and toasted
1/2 pound Brazil nuts, shelled and chopped

Preheat oven to 400°F. Sift together flour, baking soda, salt, and cinnamon.

In a large bowl, cream butter. Add sugar gradually; continue working until smooth. Beat in eggs; stir in flour. Add fruit and nuts. Drop batter from a teaspoon onto an ungreased cookie sheet; bake for 8 minutes or until light brown.

Cracker Candy

Soda crackers
2 cubes (1 cup) butter
1 cup brown sugar
1 12-ounce package chocolate chips
Finely chopped nuts (optional)

Preheat oven to 400°F. Line a large cookie sheet with aluminum foil. Cover foil with soda crackers.

In a medium saucepan over medium heat, melt butter. Add brown sugar; bring to boil. Stir constantly for 3 minutes. Pour mixture over crackers. Bake for 4 minutes—watch closely so the candy does not scorch. Remove from oven; sprinkle chocolate chips over candy. When chocolate has melted, spread out to edges. Sprinkle finely chopped nuts over the top if desired. Allow to cool; break apart. Store in a cool place.

Peggy remembers these Christmas wreaths that Grandma Glass made. They were cute and attracted the eyes of a little girl. Grandma always cautioned the kids to not eat the silver shot because she said she didn't want them to get sick.

Grandma Glass's Christmas Wreaths

30 marshmallows
1/2 cup butter
1 teaspoon vanilla
2 teaspoons green food coloring
3 1/2 cups corn flakes

Combine marshmallows, butter, vanilla, and food coloring in the top of a double boiler. Heat over water until marshmallows and butter are melted; stir frequently. Remove from heat; gradually stir in corn flakes. Drop from teaspoon onto waxed paper. Shape into small wreaths two to three inches in diameter. Decorate with silver shot and red cinnamon candies or other small red ball-shaped candies.

My favorite candy is from a recipe my mother-in-law introduced to me. It is fun to make this and share it with other family members who remember this as a family tradition. Mother Glass called it:

CHRISTMAS CANDY TOFFEE

1/2 pound butter (do not substitute)
1 packed cup brown sugar
2 small chocolate bars, broken into small pieces

Butter a 7" x 11" baking dish and cover bottom with broken nutmeats (I use pecans).

In a medium saucepan, boil butter and sugar until brittle when tested in cold water. Stir well while boiling. Pour the boiling candy over the nutmeats in the pan. (Do not beat this candy.) Sprinkle chocolate pieces over the mixture while it is still very hot. When melted, spread chocolate over the candy. Cut while warm or break into pieces when cold. Store in airtight container.

AUTHOR'S NOTE: I often do not use any chocolate and just break it when cold like you do peanut brittle.

Darrel and our daughters love to spend time together making candy and other treats. One that we all enjoy is this recipe for microwave peanut brittle that Darrell makes each year.

MICROWAVE PEANUT BRITTLE

1 cup raw peanuts
  (must be raw, unsalted peanuts)
1 cup granulated sugar
1/2 cup light corn syrup
1/8 teaspoon salt
1 teaspoon butter or margarine
1 teaspoon vanilla
Coconut (optional)

In a 1 1/2-quart casserole, stir together peanuts, sugar, corn syrup, salt. Cook 8 minutes on high in microwave oven, stirring well after 4 minutes. Stir in butter and vanilla. Return to microwave; cook on high for 2 minutes. Add 1 teaspoon baking soda; stir in quickly. *Mixture will be light and foamy.* Immediately pour onto lightly greased 10" x 15" inch baking sheet; spread very thin. If desired, coconut may be sprinkled on top. When cool, break into pieces. Store in airtight container.

Christmas is for kids . . .

"I like Christmas because we get to sing Christmas songs and bake Christmas cookies. We also get to see all of our families. It is fun! One of my favorite things is decorating the tree."

–Tiffany Glass, Fourth Grade

Stories touch our hearts and entertain us on quiet evenings together.

A Ribbon in Her Hair

Tessie was so excited. Her favorite time of the year was here. It was time for the Christmas program. Her classroom was filled with energy as the children practiced their parts for the program. Teacher was patient and kind as she encouraged each child. It was a wonderful time for Tessie.

Mother felt that Tessie was never going to stop talking. Every minute she was home her enthusiasm was bubbling over. "Mom, just think! I am going to be Mother Goose! That is the lead part of the whole program. Aren't I lucky!"

"Yes, Tessie. You are lucky. I am proud of you. You must study your part carefully and do well. Your teacher has entrusted you with this big role. She is expecting a lot of you, but I know that you can do it and she knows this too. She has confidence in you."

Tessie faithfully studied her script and learned pages of dialogue. Not only did she learn her own part but the parts of the other characters also. Her mind seemed to soak everything in like a sponge. She didn't realize it but her teacher knew this was one of her talents and was taking advantage of her natural ability. Another talent her teacher was aware of was the ability Tessie had to speak clearly and distinctly with enough volume for the audience to hear her and understand what she was saying. This role in the program was going to put her abilities to the test. They were going to present their program in the Town Hall without any microphones or sound system support.

Each day at school was exciting. The children faithfully practiced and worked on their parts, memorizing their lines.

Tessie was a little "worry wort" and became very anxious, afraid a blizzard would come and prevent her from getting to town and performing her part. With her little heart full of excitement, she talked to the Lord and begged Him to let them have nice weather.

Good weather for the evening prevailed and Tessie and her family were at the Town Hall early so Tessie could be with the other children as they did their last minute preparations for the program.

Dressed in a lovely red plaid Christmas dress her mom had sewn for her, Tessie felt pretty and happy. It was time to begin the program and Tessie proudly walked to the front of the auditorium and up onto the stage. They sang their concert of carols and then took their places in the audience as the "upper grade kids" sang their Christmas songs.

Tessie still was all excited because she knew the best was yet to come. She would get to play the part of

Mother Goose. In her mind she kept going over her lines so she would not forget them. Then she heard some ladies, who were sitting behind her, talking. Not thinking too much about it she ignored them, until she heard one lady say: "If she only had a ribbon in her hair."

Tessie wondered who they were talking about and quickly looked at the other girls. She saw they all had ribbons in their hair. Then she realized, she was the only one without a ribbon in her hair. In all her short life, she had had very few ribbons and pretty things. She knew her mother had done well to make her a new dress with the family's limited budget. Tessie was happy and content to have a new dress. Her little heart was crushed by the thoughtless remark made by someone she really didn't know. She began to wonder if she was good enough to go on with the program when she didn't have a ribbon in her hair.

Thankfully, Tessie's parents had given her a resiliency that helped her bounce back from this type of pain. She decided she couldn't let her teacher down. She had a responsibility to help make the program a success.

The time came for her to go backstage and be dressed in her costume. As she put on her long black dress and bonnet she realized it didn't make any difference if she had a ribbon or not. Seated in her rocking chair she began the play by saying her lines: "Alack and Alas! Oh, dreary me! Here it is Christmas Eve and I am all alone. None of my children are home. It will be a lonely evening for me."

The program continued with Mother Goose being surprised as Jack and Jill, Little Boy Blue, Jack Horner, Peter, Peter Pumpkin Eater, The Old Woman in the Shoe and her children, and all the rest of the characters came home to celebrate Christmas with Mother Goose. They had planned a surprise for her. The spirits of

Mother Goose were lifted as she greeted each one of her children. Mother Goose had a very special Christmas with her family gathered around. Playing her role, Tessie too felt her spirits lift.

Mother and Dad and her brothers and sisters all clapped loudly along with the rest of the audience. The program was a success and Tessie was praised for doing so well.

Going home, Tessie asked her mom, "Why did that lady say that? Was I supposed to have a ribbon in my hair?" Mother soothed her hurting heart and wept a little because she couldn't give her children all of the things that other children had.

The love they shared carried Tessie and her family through that moment of pain and many more times of trouble as the years went on. As she grew older she learned that it really didn't matter if she had a ribbon in her hair if she had beauty in her heart.

Christmas is for kids . . .

"Christmas is fun because I like to see the presents under the tree. It's fun to try and guess what is in all the packages. I like to see the expressions on people's faces when they open up a present from me. I also like to finally see what all the presents under the tree really were."

–Becky Wicklund, Fourth Grade

Home is where our family is.

A Word from the Glass Kids

I asked each of our three children to share a little of what Christmas at home meant to them when they were children and their thoughts and feelings of the holiday. The girls wrote more than Rod who sometimes is a man of few words.

From Peggy:

Mom asked, "What does Christmas mean to you? What memories does it bring to mind?" That was an easy question to answer. For me Christmas means two things, home and family. No matter where I have lived during my life, Christmas always means going "home-home." Where I live is my home, but "home-home" is going home to our family farm where Dad and Mom live. Home is where our family is. Without those two ingredients, Christmas wouldn't be much of anything to me.

To me, Christmas isn't really just a day or two anymore, it's more the season. It's coming home to make fudge and other candy. It's making doughnuts, because I only make doughnuts with my sister at Christmastime. It's teasing Dad and Mom about the lutefisk and trying to get the new family members to try it. It's coming home to shake the presents under the Christmas tree and to sneak presents into people's stockings on Christmas Day early in the morning. It's shopping all year to find just the right present for someone. It's having corn casserole for Christmas Eve supper. It's checking out all of Mom's Christmas trees to see where the ornaments are this year. It's teasing Dad and Darin about being outdoor lighting fanatics. It's having Dad wonder if "all the people" have come home to Judy's and my Christmas villages. Christmas is listening to our favorite Christmas records, playing games, watching "White Christmas" and just being home with family.

When we were little, we had such fun on Christmas Eve when we were all together. We had fun opening our gifts. One year, my cousin Randy and I each got a rocking/jumping horse. I named mine King and he was ridden hard and long for years to come.

Grandma always made little green Christmas wreath cookies with silver balls on them. I can still hear her telling Randy and me not to eat the little silver balls because they would make us sick.

Christmas Day was always a day full of company. We always had family and friends for dinner. Grandpa and Great-Great Uncle Roy would come, Auntie Agnes and Uncle Ordeen. Some years Alma would come.

Alma was Grandma's cousin and a very prim and proper retired schoolteacher. She always made us giggle, because she wanted to call Judy "Judith." We giggled when she told us the story of the first time she cooked dried prunes and how they kept expanding and expanding. We giggled when she checked out Mom's spices and said, "By golly, I have all the spices you do!" We were never allowed to use that word and thought it was funny because a grownup said a forbidden word.

It was so fun when they were all in the house because we heard so many stories about when they grew up, when Dad was growing up and all of the fun they had. They taught us so much about our family heritage and the people in our family. They also taught us so much about families and about love.

Christmas also came to our school. When we were in elementary school, we practiced many hours on our Christmas program. I was so excited the year I was to be the narrator and had to learn "The Night Before Christmas" by heart. In junior high, we were in the band and choir with teachers who appreciated Christmas music. One year our band director, Mr. Dahle, told us we sounded so good that we were going to raise the gym roof. During the concert, we kept looking up to see if the roof would even wiggle a little. In academy, our choir performed the Messiah and to this day I can still remember the alto parts. Mr. Leukert passed on his appreciation for good music and made learning parts fun.

Rod and Dawn's family brought new life to Christmas, when Kyle and Tiffany were born. We have tried to persuade the kids to give us hints as to what is in packages but they aren't too cooperative. When Judy was little she loved to give us a good hint. For example, "It is something long and it goes around your neck." Or, "It is something that is in a bottle and it smells good."

Christmas stretches into New Year at our house. We had such fun parties on New Year's Eve. We would go to Ervin and Orlene Kiesz's house or they would come to our house. We played games, rode snowmobiles and ate all kinds of food. We rarely watched TV. I was quite old before I realized there was a ball that dropped in Times Square each year. I always thought New Year's Eve meant being with the Kiesz family and the rest of our friends.

It was a sad Christmas the year Grandma died and we did not have her with us. Grandpa spent Christmas Eve alone after that. He told me it was because he wanted to stay home and think about Grandma and all the fun Christmas Eves they had spent together. He said it just wouldn't be the same without Grandma laughing beside him and loving him.

I always miss my Grandma on Christmas Eve. But it is with happy memories because I know I was loved. From then on I had an important job to do for Grandpa every year. I was his secretary and wrote the names on all of the Christmas gift envelopes for everyone. He always made me feel special.

The year after Grandpa died was very lonely. It took years to adjust to not having him with us. Many of the people we spent Christmas with when we were kids are now gone from our lives and I miss them. They made my life rich with memories of love and good times.

Christmas time also brings Dad and Mom's wedding anniversary. Rod and I always got permission to go shopping after piano lessons to find a card for them. (Judy was too little to join in this shopping expedition.) We always tried to stay away from the mushy ones! We thought we saw plenty of "mushy stuff" at home and didn't need to buy a card with the same stuff on it.

One year Rod and I decided to bake them an anniversary cake. Grandpa was babysitting us while they went out to supper and we baked away. It was a good chocolate cake! One year we bought them a blue glass vase. The vase part is on top of a long stem of glass. We had the store put it in several bags. Rod and I hung onto each other and tippy-toed along the street on the ice to the car. We didn't want to fall and break it.

FROM ROD:

What I remember most about Christmas is that it was nearly always the same. Each year we observed the traditions our family had established. I liked this because it made Christmas a warm, loving and secure time. It signified stability to us as children.

Having our grandparents, aunts, uncles and other family members come, made Christmas Day a special day. I liked our traditional Christmas Eve supper and like all children, was anxious to get to the gift opening time. It always seemed to take a long time for the grown-ups to get the dishes done and the food put away.

We got excited when it was time for Santa Claus to come. We followed the same tradition that my Dad's family had followed. Santa came and knocked on the windows and we would run from window to window and follow him around the house and finally he would come in with little gifts for us in his pack, which really was a pillowcase. We thought it was really fun, even when knew who Santa was.

Some things that happened when I was quite young made lasting memories. I remember the Christmas our cousin David came home from Vietnam and seeing him sit on the couch in his uniform. Memories are an important part of Christmas to me.

One year our cousin Randy and I begged for toy snowmobiles that were battery operated. We thought they would be the most wonderful gift. Dad didn't want us to recognize what was in the boxes so he packed them in a much bigger box. Around the snowmobile, he packed wood blocks so when I opened the box all I saw was the many blocks of wood. I had to dig through the wood blocks to find the toy snowmobile. I remember I got an Arctic Cat snowmobile and Randy got a Polaris—just like the ones our dads drove.

When Dawn and I married we combined the traditions that we both grew up with and added new ones of our own. We began the tradition of opening some of our gifts with just our children before the rest of the family comes. We decided to do this because Kyle and Tiffany would get so excited they wouldn't take time to look at their gifts and remember who they were from. This has become a meaningful tradition to which we all look forward. Our kids also enjoy the tradition of baking and decorating cookies as a family project.

From Judy:

Christmas! The very thought of it brings many wonderful memories to mind: Christmas dinner shared with family and friends; the delight of my family as they open their gifts that have been chosen with great care; Santa Claus' visits; the picture-taking ritual; how Christmas Eve supper seemed to last so long and the dishes took forever to wash before we could finally open presents; Christmas morning stockings with hard candy covered in lint from the sock; packages that gurgle and tick; Tartex and tuna fish; watching "White Christmas" with Dad commenting on how well they dance without ever having practiced. All of these memories are special, but I think the thing I enjoy the most about Christmas is the anticipation.

The anticipation of Christmas seems to start the day after Christmas when we venture out to hit the after-Christmas sales. We begin looking for gifts and decorations for the next Christmas. As the year progresses, I continue to keep my eyes open for the "perfect" gifts for my family, something special and meaningful, that they will treasure and enjoy. (The annual Far Side calendars for my brother and brother-in-law.)

When the end of July or beginning of August arrives, I book my tickets home for Christmas. I do this at this time for two reasons: First, so I can get the flights I need before they are filled and Second, so I can look forward to and know exactly when I will see my family next.

I try to have my Christmas shopping finished before Thanksgiving, because December is always such a busy time of year. Plus, I don't enjoy fighting the crowds while shopping. Having my shopping done makes December less hectic and allows me more time to enjoy the Christmas festivities.

Finally the day arrives when I get to go home. It is so much fun when I arrive home. I spend a few minutes checking Dad's outdoor lighting job, checking each room of the house to see if Mom has all of the Christmas decorations out and in their places, then checking the Christmas treats looking for Mom's popcorn balls and Dad's "Always Fail Fudge." I ask Dad when he wants to dip the Hi Ho crackers, sandwiched with peanut butter in the middle, in melted almond bark. I look forward to reading all of the Christmas cards from family and friends.

Then there is the tree with all of the presents wrapped and arranged at its base. I spend a few minutes wondering which packages are mine and what treasures each wrapped box holds.

Over the years, we (my siblings and I) have developed quite a talent for "present shaking." "Present shaking" involves more than shaking. It is determining the size of the package, the weight, how the weight is distributed, if it makes any noise or gives off any odors. The kind of box and wrapping paper are additional important clues. Also, it is helpful to notice if anyone else has a package the same size and shape. Often heard comments at this time of year include: "Don't shake that box!" "Mom, Peggy's peeking." "If you're not good you won't get any presents." (Remember, this is being told to "children" who are all over 30!) "Don't look in there! Remember it is Christmas!"

One of my favorite Christmas memories is sitting in the living room on Friday night with only the Christmas tree lights on as my sister played Christmas carols on the piano. My family shakes a few presents, looks the tree over, locating various ornaments, sharing their stories and talking of Christmases past. What I enjoy, most of all, is just being together. The rush of the day is laid aside and time is spent together as a family.

Christmas Eve finally arrives. As is our tradition, we have to eat supper then do all of the dishes before we can finally open presents. When at last it is time, we all seem to want to make it last as long as possible. The presents are passed out to each person with a little confusion over the names of Dawn and Darin which look very similar when written in cursive, especially to Kyle and Tiffany.

The anticipation of choosing which present to open first builds. Do you open first the one you think you know what it is or do you open the one you don't have a clue as to what is in the package? Stories are shared as gifts are opened about where they were purchased or the difficulty in locating that special present.

We relish the precious moments drawing them out as long as possible—practicing patience. Enjoying receiving specially pondered over gifts and giving carefully chosen or created gifts is Christmas to me. Anticipating each receiver's reaction and laughing at the banter such as "Does this come installed?" or "So that's what happened to the canned goods." Or "Here, Grandpa, let me help you with that" as four willing little hands reach out to help rip off the paper. It's all a special part of the evening.

As another Christmas Eve comes to an end, we look

forward to Christmas Day and the fun it brings. Christmas stockings, complete with the traditional ornament, dinner with family, more relaxing and sharing and maybe some games. Christmas and anticipation just seem to go together.

When it's all over, we will look back with warm hearts full of treasured memories of family and friends and home.

As I read these thoughts of our children, I know that the practice we have had through the years of observing family traditions has been worth the extra effort and work. Our family has always enjoyed celebrating Christmas together. It is a time of the year when we try to keep the days free of heavy jobs and activities that will take us away from home. It is more than a day. It is a season. When the children were in academy and college we always wanted to be free to spend as much time as possible with them so we planned ahead to make their vacation times a time when we also took time off from work and spent time together as a family. We still plan for the holiday season to be more relaxed and free of outside activities. It is truly a season of family life enjoyed to the fullest at our house.

Christmas is for kids . . .

"Christmas means making decorations, coloring or drawing Christmas pictures, playing in the deep snow and making snowmen or snow angels. I also like making cookies and playing games. I think of a lot of things at Christmastime. Christmas is probably my favorite time of the year, also the busiest."

–Courtney Tasche, Fifth Grade

Hearts filled with gratitude go home for Christmas.

Heartfelt Memories

Reading through the many responses from the people whom I surveyed, I was impressed at the amount of gratitude expressed for the homes in which they grew up.

Maude Buchholz, who has lived a rich and full life for 90 years, expressed this well:

"I think back to when I was a child. Our home was a home where we didn't have much of this world's goods but there was always at least one gift for all of us at Christmas. I know now that my mother spent many long hours at night making them. It was generally clothes, but I remember one year when my sister and I each got a rag doll. Oh, how precious they were to us. The boys were happy over the caps and mittens that Mom had made for them.

"Mom and Dad both taught us to live our lives in a Christian way. As I look back on those days so long ago, I am thankful for parents who taught me to be honest in all things and live my life as a Christian and to keep God in our lives. We are now scattered here and there over the states but we always tried to come home for Christmas, even if it was over the telephone."

Pat Wangsnes wrote:

"I grew up during the depression years in Port Arthur, Ontario. Money was scarce and we lived with very few luxuries. To us the important things were family and friends. Thinking of those times brings a flood of happy memories of a time when we were truly blessed. We had a mother and father who truly loved and cared for us. We looked forward to Christmas with great anticipation even though we knew most of the time the only gifts we would receive were necessary items that mother made.

"Mother baked my dad's favorite cookies—molasses—and almond refrigerator cookies—which were her favorite. We kids loved them all. We also had the traditional nuts in the shell that we would shell in the evenings while Dad entertained us by telling funny stories. We loved our annual walk downtown with our dad on Christmas Eve before supper to see the Christmas lights and displays in the stores.

"Two young girls from Saskatchewan who worked as domestic workers in our town spent a lot of days with us after church services. They always joined us at Christmas. We all loved to sit around and sing hymns and Christmas carols."

Christmas is about love of family. Beginning with the

family of Mary, Joseph, and Baby Jesus, we find a record of the love that a poor family experienced those many years ago. Today, we have our families where we are privileged to invite Jesus to come and be our Guest. Making the Lord Jesus a constant part of our life enhances our families and brings untold blessings to our homes. Our hearts are filled with gratitude for the wonderful Gift that was given to us. That Gift is the reason we celebrate Christmas.

May your hearts go home for Christmas as you remember the blessings of your home and family. Cherish the memories of the years in the past and most importantly, look forward to the memories still to be made. May all of your Christmas celebrations be blessed with love, peace, joy, and happiness and may they be filled with the presence of our Lord.

Recipe Index